MY RESCUE DOG

MY RESCUE DOG

A PRACTICAL GUIDE TO PROVIDING A FOREVER HOME

DAVID ALDERTON

LORENZ BOOKS

Contents

INTRODUCTION	**6**	Getting to know your rescue dog	46
		What dogs tell you	48
SO YOU WANT A RESCUE DOG?	**8**	Safeguarding your home and garden	50
Why do dogs end up homeless?	10	Car safety	52
Street dogs	12	Veterinary considerations	54
The different types of dog	14	Essential equipment	56
Becoming a doggy detective!	16		
Adopting a puppy	18	**BRINGING YOUR RESCUE DOG HOME**	**58**
Adopting an older dog	20	Paperwork practicalities	60
Hard to re-home dogs	22	The first few days	62
Accessing help for hard to re-home dogs	24	The importance of house-training	64
Assessing your commitment	26	Another pet in the house	66
Assessing your lifestyle	28	Meeting visitors	68
FINDING YOUR IDEAL COMPANION	**32**	**A DEVELOPING RELATIONSHIP**	**70**
Beginning the search	34	Beginning training	72
Obtaining a dog from another country	36	Ongoing training	74
Contacting the rescue centre	38	Regular exercise	76
Questions to ask	40	Letting your dog off the leash	78
The first meeting	42	Reacting to the great outdoors	80
The assessor's visit	44	How technology can help	82

Toys for your dog	84	Coping with visitors	132
Sporting possibilities	86	Some concerns of modern living	134
Feeding	88	Travel precautions	136
Reviewing your dog's diet	90	Outdoor concerns	140
Weight and obesity	92	Aggression issues	144
Grooming your dog	94	Behavioural or health concerns	148
Your dog and holidays	96		
Issues with ageing	98	**HELPING OUT**	**152**
Coping with disabilities	102	Volunteering	154
First aid for your dog	104	Hands-on help	156
Natural treatments for chronic pain	106	Fostering	158
Acupuncture for pain relief	108	Permanent residents	161
Natural treatments to aid recovery	110		
Natural ways to calm a nervous dog	112	**TRAINING**	**162**
		Mastering the basics	164
TROUBLESHOOTING	**114**	Safety considerations	166
Issues around food	116	Controlling your dog's movements	168
Problems around handling your dog	120	Distance, duration and distractions	170
Control issues	122	Phasing out rewards	171
Garden play concerns	124		
Separation anxiety	128	Index/Acknowledgements	172

Introduction

Although domestic dogs are seen as our closest companions in the animal world, many sadly fall on hard times and need help – otherwise they are likely to be destroyed. The description of 'rescue dog' is used to refer to a dog of any age or background that has ended up homeless, irrespective of the underlying cause. It has been taken into care and will be looking for a new home.

Dogs can find themselves in this situation for a wide variety of reasons. Financial issues, family breakdown and bereavement are some of the more common causes why owners can no longer look after their pets, while in other cases, real or perceived behavioural issues are responsible.

The scale of the problem may not always be obvious, but it remains

▲ *Not all dogs are fortunate enough to have a loving home for life. Rescues therefore cater for individuals of all ages.*

▼ *Dogs from rescue centres can develop into lively, affectionate and playful pets – they simply need to be given the opportunity.*

very real. It is a stark fact that, according to official figures, over 110,000 stray or abandoned dogs are taken off the streets every year in the UK, with countless thousands of these being unwanted and so ending up being euthanized. Around five million homeless dogs pass into the care of approximately 3,500 rescue shelters in the USA. The total number of strays on the streets in the United States is even higher, with the figure likely to be around 70 million, according to some estimates.

Fewer than 10% of these dogs have been neutered, and, inevitably, there are dogs rounded up and passed on to shelters that have spent their whole life on the streets, providing a particular challenge for potential adopters. It's a staggering fact that potentially, a single unspayed bitch and her offspring can be responsible for some 67,000 puppies over a

six-year period. The key to making a major impact on the number of stray dogs roaming the streets is neutering. This is why all rescues insist on dogs in their care being neutered before being rehomed, aiming to send a message at least, even if not providing a solution.

The consequences for the rescue dog

The outlook for shelter dogs is frequently bleak and uncertain. While some organizations such as Dogs Trust, which is the largest dogs' welfare charity in the UK, have a policy that dogs brought to them will not be put to sleep, the fact is that about half of all dogs that find their way into shelters in the USA for

◄ *Greyhounds are one of the most common breeds to be found in rescue centres. These dogs develop into very loving individuals that settle well in domestic surroundings.*

example will end up being euthanized. This works out at 5,500 dogs being destroyed every single day – amounting to an alarming tally of more than two million over the course of a year.

This figure is shocking, and could so easily be prevented with more responsible ownership. Thankfully, however, there is a growing groundswell of opinion amongst dog-lovers to actively seek homeless dogs as pets, easing the toll on rescue shelters – a trend that has been highlighted and promoted by popular television programmes and personal accounts of living with rescue dogs, as portrayed over recent years in books and films.

In addition, there is a wide range of different organizations that exist to help dogs in need, aiming to find new 'forever' homes for those that pass into their care. These may be national organizations, local groups or even individuals, all working to assist rescue dogs in need of help, with many being charities.

Getting it right

While starting out with any dog is not something to be undertaken lightly, taking on a rescue dog can prove to be even more challenging. But when it works out, you really do have a friend for life! For owners who may be unprepared, however, this approach to dog-ownership can become a major heartache rather than a joy – and is likely to prove to be much harder than starting out with a puppy, in the initial stages particularly.

Homeless dogs are now being moved across the European continent and they are even being brought from countries further afield, such as China, by rescue organizations. But if you acquire a rescue dog independently, making all the arrangements to bring it back yourself, do bear in mind that you may well have no support with your dog when you get home, whereas rescue centres can provide help and ongoing advice. Your new pet may well have come from a totally different environment, with little or no history as to its background, thus creating potential problems for you.

Although it is certainly not possible to predict what issues a rescue dog may or may not have, this book takes a practical and down-to-earth approach to the subject, throughout, recognizing that rescue dogs generally have particular needs, and that great care must be taken pairing up a dog and owner.

▼ *Building a bond with a rescue dog can be particularly enjoyable, as you strike up a rapport with your new companion.*

CHAPTER ONE

SO YOU WANT A RESCUE DOG?

Human instincts being what they are, it is quite natural to want to help where possible. When choosing a dog as a pet, that feeling extends very much to puppies or older dogs that have had a rough start in life or find themselves homeless because of unfortunate circumstances. With increased media coverage of this issue over recent years, there is growing awareness of the frighteningly large number of dogs that pass into the care of rescue organizations on an annual basis, many of which are likely to end up being put to sleep, if they cannot be re-homed.

It is therefore an obvious starting point to think about the possibility of choosing a homeless individual to become your forever companion, rather than seeking out a dog from a breeder. Yet you need to consider this option with particular care and be clear in your own mind about what could be involved in going down this path. Just as in the case of people who have been unfortunate enough to suffer serious trauma in their lives, so dogs too can be badly affected by their past life experiences, in ways that may not even be immediately apparent.

Every case is individual, and while this may mean that some individuals settle quickly and with few, if any, discernible problems, the impact of other past experiences can be lifelong. The lasting adverse effects can be reduced through careful and caring management, however, meaning that you can still end up with a very loyal and loving canine companion, which in turn makes the overall process exceedingly rewarding.

◄ *Dogs that have spent their entire lives living on the street are typically the most challenging to settle successfully into domestic life.*

Why do dogs end up homeless?

Unfortunately, it sometimes turns out that sadly, despite careful thought and the best intentions, not everyone who sets out to obtain a canine companion for life can fulfil this pledge. Over the course of more than a decade, some people's lives can change significantly, and this may impact on their ability to continue to look after a pet dog.

Cost considerations

Financial issues can also result in dogs finding themselves homeless. It is important to realise that keeping a pet dog will prove to be a relatively costly undertaking. Food can be a significant expense, with larger dogs having bigger appetites than small individuals and proving more of a commitment as a result.

Health care and veterinary insurance costs also need to be considered, while what to do with your dog if you go away on holiday and any day-care costs, plus specialist grooming and dog-walking services, may have to be added to the overall total, in addition to the initial outlay on equipment such as coats, toys, and beds.

There are numerous reasons why a once much-wanted dog ends up being taken to a rescue centre to be re-homed.

Changes in personal circumstances

It may be the case that a couple or young family bring home a cute puppy that at first seems just perfect but no-one has really taken on board how much time and attention a dog needs to flourish. Work or childcare commitments can make it seem impossible to attend to their growing dog's needs as well.

Family breakdowns and moves, especially overseas, may also impact on the ability to care for a dog, although it is often easier to relocate with dogs than has been the case in

▲ *Personal problems such as an owner's health issues or family breakdown can leave dogs homeless.*

the past, especially as specialist shipping companies provide a comprehensive service to many destinations worldwide.

Then of course, some owners, especially those living on their own, may become too frail or ill to look after a dog, and there is no family relative or friend who can assist. If an owner dies, this too can leave a dog without anyone to care for it, so that it ends up being passed to a rescue organization to be re-homed.

▶ *Large dogs have correspondingly bigger appetites, are stronger and generally need more exercise.*

Behavioural issues

Unfortunately, not everyone is entirely truthful when handing over a dog to the care of a rescue organization. People sometimes

▶ *Some behavioural issues, including aggressive triggers, may only emerge in rescue dogs over the course of time.*

claim that they are having to make this decision for economic reasons when the underlying reason is a behavioural issue. The difficulty is that this might not be immediately apparent, based on the dog's day-to-day behaviour. It could be that the dog becomes very aggressive when mail is dropping through the letterbox for example, or reacts very badly during a thunderstorm, soiling in the home, or perhaps more commonly, proves destructive around the home when left alone.

It may not be possible for rescue centres to determine certain behavioural issues easily either, unless the dog is being fostered with a temporary carer, rather than being kept in kennels. Worse still in such cases is that it is not uncommon for the issue to become more severe, as the dog's level of uncertainty rises with the increasing number of major changes in its life, as it is passed repeatedly from one owner to another rescue centre and so on. This creates a chain of anxiety in its mind, adding to the dog's sense of insecurity and often worsening the problem.

Rescues centres do try to prevent this cycle of dogs passing back and forth, firstly by trying to identify any underlying behavioural issues that

the dog may have, based on the previous owner's account and their own observations. Obviously, knowing there is an issue of this type makes it much easier to address.

Health concerns

There can also be a variety of dogs handed into rescue centres because of underlying health issues that their previous owners could not manage successfully, for one reason or another. Rather than being put to sleep, the dog was therefore passed over to the rescue. Cases of this type can often involve epilepsy, which is more likely to be encountered in some breeds than others.

Seizures or fits can start at a relatively young age, from about six months of age onwards. It can appear very alarming, particularly if you are

▶ *Dogs that are teething and/or bored often become destructive, and this can lead to them being discarded.*

unaware of what happens under these circumstances, as an affected dog will collapse, and most evidently, will start paddling with its feet, lying on its side. It may well lose control of its bowels and bladder during this period too.

Another common medical reason that results in dogs passing into care is when an individual is diagnosed with *diabetes mellitus* and needs regular injections of insulin. These must be given once or twice daily. Not everyone feels able to inject their pet, and this fear of needles plays a major part in diabetic dogs being given over to rescue centres.

Street dogs

Not every dog is fortunate enough to be taken to a rescue centre. Some dogs are simply abandoned by their previous owners and left to fend for themselves. Other dogs may have been born on the streets and have never known human companionship. It may not seem particularly important why a dog ends up homeless as it needs help, but this can be crucial for successful re-homing.

The most significant thing that is lacking with a street dog will almost certainly be its previous history, which can prove to be a vital consideration when it comes to integrating the dog successfully into a home with you.

This is especially likely nowadays, as some dogs will have crossed international borders in search of new homes, being brought originally from countries far away from the rescue centres where they have ended up. Local volunteers take in individuals that need help, and nurse them back to health as far as possible, before sending them on to find permanent homes elsewhere, with the necessary tests, vaccinations and paperwork completed.

▼ *Many street dogs bear scars as the result of past fights or accidents, and may have a legacy of chronic pain in some cases.*

There is usually a significant lack of information, however, about the individual background of such dogs. It may well be that in many cases, they are simply street dogs, which have spent most if not all their lives living in this harsh and dangerous environment having to fend for themselves. Many such individuals come to the attention of the rescue organizations because they have been injured, often in a collision with a vehicle.

A nervous nature

With dogs of this type, aside from any physical injury that may affect their subsequent mobility, it is important to bear in mind that frequently, they will have had little direct contact with people at any stage through their lives. There is a key period in a puppy's development, known as the socialization phase, which lasts from 4–12 weeks of life.

▲ *Dogs used to living on the streets will have developed an instinctive wariness of people, which means they will be nervous.*

This is the period when puppies need to be exposed to key stimuli, such as human contact, if they are to grow up without being nervous.

As a result, deprived of such contact, young dogs of this type will almost certainly be shy by nature, particularly with strangers. Therefore, you will need to be much more patient getting to know an anxious street dog and winning its confidence. Be prepared as well for your pet to be more nervous when meeting other people with you.

Puppies born on the streets will still learn from their litter mates under these circumstances, in terms of key behaviours such as play and restraining their biting power, and they will not be nervous around other dogs. Yet an important consideration to bear in mind is that they will not have been house-trained at all. Again, this should not ultimately be an issue, as it should be

▲ *Puppies born on the streets should settle much faster than adults, if they can be brought into care and socialized early in life.*

possible to train your new dog accordingly, but it will take more time than with a puppy reared at home where the progress has already

▼ *Street dogs are usually talented escape-artists. Checking the boundaries of your property are secure is vital.*

been started. Equally, it can also be more difficult and even frustrating, but it is achievable with a combination of both patience and keen observational skills on your part, to pre-empt any issues arising.

Age determination

Working out the age of a dog that has been homeless for any length of time is not always easy, simply because they may often show signs of their tough existence, causing them to appear older than may be the case. With younger individuals however, their teeth can be a useful indicator, but only for a relatively limited period.

Dogs have a set of 28 deciduous (or 'milk' teeth), which start to be replaced by their permanent teeth from about five months of age onwards. This process will take about two months, by which time all 42 permanent teeth should have

erupted. After this point, wear on the teeth, which may be a useful indicator for household pets, is of little value, given that chipped teeth for example are more common in street dogs.

Life expectancy

The lifespan of street dogs is typically measured in just a few years, because of the constant hazards, ranging from debilitating parasitic infections, such as mange, to traffic dangers, combined with the ever-present threat of starvation. By way of comparison, the average lifespan of a pet dog has risen considerably over recent decades and may possibly reach the high teens in the case of small dogs, which are naturally longer-lived than big individuals. However, provided that a street dog is in good general health when you acquire it, then its lifespan should not be affected by its earlier experiences.

The different types of dog

Most people heading in search of a rescue dog have a rather preconceived notion of the type of dog that they are searching for, although if the truth be told, this frequently changes as they start looking in earnest. Dogs have distinctive, individual personalities, helping to explain to some extent why they can become such an important part of our lives.

There are often misunderstandings about the different types of dogs that can be found in rescue centres. Many are what are simply called 'mutts', which are dogs that bear no clear resemblance to any particular breed. They are the result of random matings over several generations, but sadly, fashions in dog-breeding are also reflected in the various dogs passing in to the care of rescues.

Designer dogs

The big trend over recent years has been the emergence of so-called designer dogs. These are the result of crossings between two different breeds, with the resulting puppies varying widely in appearance.

Such dogs were originally bred in Australia, with the intention of

▲ *The type of dogs that end up in rescues will generally mirror those that are popular amongst dog-owners.*

creating guide dogs that were hypo-allergenic, and therefore suitable for allergy sufferers. Poodles were used with the sole aim of introducing this feature, as they do not shed their coats and are an intelligent, adaptable breed.

The resulting crosses with Labrador retrievers became known as Labradoodles, although the plan did not work out entirely in practice. This is because people can become allergic to tiny skin particles or 'dander', just as much as the coat itself. Furthermore, some Labradoodles shed hair too.

Poodles have remained central to the more popular designer dogs created as pets, such as Cavipoos (Cavalier King Charles spaniel x poodle) or cockapoos (cocker spaniel x poodle). Although standard poodles have been used in the creation of Labradoodles, smaller poodle breeds have been preferred in these two newer crosses. There are now many other designer crosses, such as Italjacks (Italian greyhound x Jack Russell terrier), which have no links to poodles.

▼ *Labradoodles were the original 'designer dog'. Today, the focus is more on smaller, companion breeds.*

▼ *An Italjack puppy. Knowing the parent breeds provides insight into the temperament and size of such crosses.*

▶ *Staffordshire bull terriers, 'Staffies', are popular generally, and frequently find their way into rescues. They are strong dogs for their size, but can make very loyal companions.*

Unfortunately, the huge increase in the popularity and numbers of designer dogs being produced has inevitably resulted in some individuals subsequently ending up in the care of rescue centres, in need of new homes.

Pure-bred dogs

There are often misunderstandings around pure-bred dogs, with the term 'pedigree' being used interchangeably with this description. Although a pedigree dog will be pure-bred, there is no guarantee that a pure-bred will be a pedigree. To be a pedigree dog, the individual needs to be registered with a national kennel club and to have the correct paperwork (indicating its pedigree, typically revealing top champion examples of the breed in its bloodline).

Simply crossing two pure-bred dogs of the same breed together does not result in pedigree offspring, even though all the puppies will be of similar appearance and will certainly be recognizable as belonging to that breed. They will not have the same prize-winning show ancestry, which takes years of dedicated breeding, that typifies pedigree dogs of the same breed.

If a pedigree dog passes into the care of a rescue centre though, the accompanying paperwork remains with the centre when the dog is re-homed. This ensures anonymity for those involved.

RACING GREYHOUNDS

One type of dog sadly encountered very commonly in rescues centres is the greyhound. These dogs are bred in large numbers for racing purposes, but the vast majority turn out to be unsuccessful on the track, with only a small percentage being retained for breeding purposes once their racing days are over.

The reality of living with a rescued greyhound is very different from what many people assume. The first misconception is that they require lots of exercise. Greyhounds are bred to sprint, rather than running over long distances, so that they do not need a rural environment.

They are gentle, affectionate dogs by nature, yet they do retain their strong hunting instincts. As a result, they should therefore be fitted with a muzzle when taken out so there is no risk that your pet will chase and overpower a much smaller dog, mistaking it for the hare.

Racing greyhounds live in kennels. House-training is therefore likely to be required, but they will soon adapt to living in domestic surroundings, loving a comfy sofa or better still, a bed! Their thin fur and almost total absence of body fat mean that they will feel the cold readily, and as in the case of other similar breeds, such as whippets and Italian greyhounds, they all need a coat or special jumper to wear, maybe even indoors in cold weather.

▲ *Ex-racing greyhounds often need new homes. They will frequently settle well in domestic surroundings.*

Becoming a doggy detective!

When confronted with a dog whose ancestry is not clear, it is useful to try to gain some insight into its likely ancestral origins. Attempting to determine the background of a particular dog based on its appearance is not always straightforward, and yet in truth, this is more than just a subject of curiosity, but can be of practical significance. This is because a dog's ancestry is likely to shape its character.

The development of pedigree dogs, notably for show purposes, is a relatively recent phenomenon that only began during the second part of the 19th century. For centuries before that, dogs were used to undertake specific tasks, such as hunting or herding farmstock, working alongside people. They developed characteristics which made them well-suited to their tasks, such as speed in the case of the greyhound, and keen scenting skills in the case of the bloodhound.

Sighthounds: a group that includes the greyhound, whippet, and saluki. Bred for speed rather than stamina, sighthounds are the athletes of the dog world, with a deep chest. They are generally quiet, and can be nervous, but are very devoted to those they know well.
Scenthounds: breeds include the beagle and different types of basset

◄ Short-legged dogs with a broad nose are likely to have a basset hound ancestry, with white areas in their coat.

hound. They possess plenty of stamina but are inclined to run off readily if an interesting scent is detected, so recall training is not very straightforward in these cases. They are more vocal than sighthounds.
Retrievers: Labradors and golden retrievers were originally bred to work on a one-to-one basis with people. They are energetic by nature, often like swimming, and are generally responsive to training.

Staffordshire bull terriers: Very loyal by nature, but strong dogs, and not always well-disposed to others of their own kind, so good socialization in the case of puppies, and on-going obedience training is very important with members of this group.
Jack Russell terriers: Just like Staffordshires, there often tends to be a high percentage of these dogs in rescue centres. They can be quite variable in appearance, in terms of

◄ The Afghan hound is an active, athletic breed with a great deal of stamina that needs plenty of exercise and a lot of grooming too.

► True companion breeds such as bichons are probably the easiest dogs to train, as they are very responsive to people.

coat type, height and markings. Curious and intelligent by nature, these terriers are often quite strong-willed.

Bichons: The most widely kept toy dogs, which have been bred over the course of centuries as companions. They are very loyal and affectionate, and often long-lived. Bichons are intelligent by nature and learn quickly in new situations. They have predominantly white, curly coats.

Some ancestry pointers

There are a few general signs that will give you insights into the type of personality that your pet may have, even if there is no clear

▶ Labrador retrievers are one of the most popular breeds worldwide today, being well-suited to homes with older children.

evidence as to its exact ancestry. These are typical characteristics that are shared with different types of dogs as indicated in each case:

• Relatively long legs and sloping back – suggests a sighthound ancestry.

◀ Staffordshire bull terriers and crosses often find themselves in need of good homes. They are powerfully built dogs and may not always agree well with others of their own kind.

• Tri-coloured, medium-sized and with relatively big ears – indicates a possible scenthound input in the dog's background.
• Quite big, with a broad head and a smooth coat – may reveal a retriever lineage.
• Medium-sized, stocky and square-faced – such dogs are of likely Staffordshire bull terrier descent.
• Short, tri-coloured and a reasonably pointed muzzle – probably descends from Jack Russell-type terrier stock, and can be either tousled in appearance, with a wire coat, or smooth-coated.
• Small, whitish with a curly coat – likely to indicate some links to the bichon breeds.

▼ Despite their small stature, Jack Russell terriers are lively, strong-willed characters with plenty of energy. They can make very devoted companions.

Adopting a puppy

When it comes to choosing between obtaining a puppy from a breeder or from a rescue, there can be differences. The first and most obvious perhaps is that if you have your heart set on a particular breed of dog, you will probably be unable to obtain it from a rescue organization. You may well find, however, delightful mongrel puppies of no set parentage, each of which is a true individual.

It is not that uncommon for stray pregnant dogs to pass into the care of rescues and give birth there. As they have been born into the care of a rescue centre, such puppies will obviously have been reared with great care and will be ready in due course to go to their forever homes, once they are about 9–10 weeks of age. This is the ideal point at which to obtain any dog, with your new companion settling in well at this stage, and it should reduce the risk of issues arising from its uncertain start in life.

▼ *Puppies which have lived on the streets may be suffering from nutritional issues and can be nervous at first.*

▲ *It may be that the puppy was born in the rescue centre and has grown up receiving plenty of attention from people.*

There may also be older puppies that need re-homing on occasions too. In general terms, the description of 'puppy' is used for a young dog that is under a year old. Unfortunately, not everyone who obtains a puppy does sufficient research, and may therefore fail to realise the level of commitment and cost involved.

Puppies go through different stages of development, and from about four months onwards, they start teething, which means that they are likely to become increasingly destructive during this phase. Items such as chair legs, other furniture

▲ *Some puppies found abandoned must be hand-reared. There are balanced milk replacers available for this purpose.*

and even carpets may be severely and irreparably damaged if you are not careful. This in turn can lead some owners to decide that they can no longer keep their pet, especially if it is causing domestic friction, leading to the young dog ending up in a rescue.

Puppy training

The extent to which puppies taken into rescues have been trained previously depends on the individual, and is something that needs to be considered, especially if you are a first-time dog-owner. A younger puppy that is ready to go to a new home will be an easier prospect than an older individual that has had little or no previous training.

Indeed, a young dog that has lived its entire life until recently roaming free on the streets or has been kept in kennels and never lived in a home will not even be house-trained. As a general guide therefore, you will need to invest more time in training an older puppy, on a fairly intensive basis at this stage, so your new companion learns what is expected.

PREVENTING CHEWING

Chewing is a problem that you will undoubtedly face, if you start out with a young puppy, but it is possible to minimize this issue. Try to supervise your puppy closely, especially while it is teething. It is also recommended to obtain some chew-type toys. Encourage your puppy to use these, to relieve the nagging pain that arises from the new teeth emerging.

You can also obtain specially formulated sprays to use, as a way of deterring your dog from being drawn to to certain items of furniture around your home. Most pet stores stock a range of sprays, and it can pay to research the brands online, or obtain several, to see which will be most effective to deter your dog.

▼ *People often do not take into consideration just how destructive puppies can prove. They need supervision and plenty of toys.*

It will therefore be very helpful if you are able to be at home for several months in the period immediately after you acquire your new pet, so you can work on the various aspects of training that will be required throughout the day.

It is quite possible for a puppy to catch up on training, but in the case of older individuals, you may need some professional assistance. Most rescues, however, carefully assess the training needs of their dogs and can advise and even give direct practical support to new owners as required.

Neutering

It is also worth bearing in mind that some behavioural problems in the case of older puppies may be related to territorial marking, with breakdowns in toilet-training in male dogs especially being caused by this reason. The situation may be improved by neutering and making sure that you clear up any accidents indoors thoroughly, so the scent will not attract your young dog back to this spot in future. If the situation continues, speak with an accredited behaviourist and your vet.

Adopting an older dog

Many of the dogs to be found in rescues are not puppies. This has both advantages and drawbacks. Older dogs can still adapt surprisingly fast in new surroundings, especially if they have lived in a home before. They are less likely to be destructive in this environment than a young puppy and may already have received some training, which will help if you are a first-time dog owner.

An older dog may have lived with one person for much of its life and it may take longer to accept you as a new owner. Some older dogs can also be very nervous, because of their past experiences, particularly when confronted by visitors coming to your home, and this can create difficulties. Much depends on an individual's background and the more information you can glean about a dog, the easier your decision will be. One of the major difficulties in adopting dogs from other countries, especially if there is a language barrier, is that you may not be able to discover very much at all about a dog that appeals to you.

▼ *Individuals kept on puppy farms for breeding purposes often end up being discarded. They may previously have lived exclusively in kennels.*

▲ *Dogs that have been used to living with people will be the easiest to settle into a new home, compared with street dogs.*

Signs of significance

It is impossible to age a dog with certainty, once it has obtained its permanent teeth, indicating that it is over six months of age. The appearance of the coat can be a useful indicator though, with the fur of many dogs often starting to turn whitish around the eyes, and particularly the muzzle, by the time they are about eight years old. This colour change will be most evident in the case of dogs which had black fur on these parts of the body. Patches of black elsewhere on the body however, on the flanks for example, do not fade in this way with age.

Nevertheless, in these individuals, other changes in appearance may become apparent. Looking in the eyes, you might detect signs of

cataracts, evident as cloudy white areas, indicating that the dog's sight has become somewhat impaired. These are quite common but will not be such a severe handicap to the dog's lifestyle as it would be to ours, simply because dogs are far less dependent on their sense of sight. They have a very keen sense of smell, as well as excellent hearing to give them a range of information about their immediate environment.

Potential ill-health

There could be other health issues of much greater concern of course, with the risk increasing in the case of older individuals. But rescue dogs are generally examined by a vet when they pass into a centre's care, and tests will have been carried out to investigate any underlying problems, if there was any cause for concern.

Veterinary tests can be very useful in a range of situations. These can

DID YOU KNOW?

Two of the oldest dogs in recent years have both been rescues. Jack, a Yorkshire terrier was rescued when he was nine years old, and lived for over a quarter of a century, dying tragically as the result of being attacked by a bigger dog when out for a walk in 2016.

Meg, who was a Jack Russell terrier, came originally from a puppy farm as a young dog back in 1991. After being rescued, she also lived for more than 25 years, before passing away in 2015.

The oldest known dog on record was an Australian cattle dog, appropriately called Bluey, who was nearly 29.5 years on his demise, although there has been a recent unverified report of a similar breed, called the kelpie, living for just over 30 years.

▲ *An Australian cattle dog with its unusual coat colouring – a member of this working breed holds the record for canine longevity.*

highlight blood parasites, such as *Babesia*, which are present in some areas of the world, and may affect dogs brought from overseas, through to kidney problems. Bad breath can be another sign of a deterioration in

kidney function, although it can also reflect dental problems too, not forgetting that both conditions can occur together!

The functioning ability of the kidneys, in terms of filtering and purifying the blood, inevitably declines with age in all dogs, but only once a significant amount of the kidney tissue has been affected will clinical signs of illness start to become evident. There is no cure with kidney disease, but the right care can ensure that affected dogs will often continue to lead a full and active life for some time.

A dog suffering from kidney failure will need to be given a modified diet, but this requirement is simplified today by the availability of specially formulated foods.

▶ *Street dogs often look older because of their hard lives, scavenging to survive on the streets. Any areas of missing fur caused by scarring are unlikely to regrow.*

Hard to re-home dogs

When it comes to advice about your chosen dog, there is no substitute for talking with the people who are caring for it daily. If they indicate that it would not be entirely suitable for you, or alternatively, suggest that there is perhaps a similar dog that would be a better choice, based on your circumstances, then you can be certain that this will be an honest assessment.

Too many rescue dogs, even with the best possible screening procedures in place, end up being recycled from what was to have been a forever home back to the rescue centre and so on. Every time, this is exceedingly disturbing for the dog and makes it harder to re-home subsequently.

Commitment required

The tragic side of this is that many dogs end up being euthanized annually, simply because they end up being tagged as unsatisfactory for re-homing. However, this is not necessarily the case – the simple truth is that people took them on before thinking through whether they could actually manage to care for them properly. When difficulties arise, as is inevitable under these

▼ *Even though a dog may appear relaxed, there can be underlying triggers from its past that mean it can become difficult to manage.*

▲ *There are inevitably some dogs in rescues that are harder to home than others, such as large dogs that need to be rehomed together.*

circumstances, so the commitment that was there tends to fade.

This can be particularly problematic if not all members of the household are equally enthusiastic about having a dog in the first place. Should there be complaints about noise from the neighbours or damage caused around the home, and one partner gets upset, blaming the dog, this can easily develop into a relationship issue as well.

In many cases, the dog then finds itself being handed back to a rescue, as a way of hopefully ensuring subsequent harmony in the household, although often, the underlying situation is much more complex.

It is therefore very important that family members – and especially the adults in the household – are all equally committed to having a dog and prepared to work together to integrate the newcomer successfully into the home, while accepting there will be problems on that path, particularly when starting with a rescue dog.

Do not be surprised if you are asked various questions on this basis when you visit the rescue centre, and whether you have kept a dog before, which will give you some insight into what to expect when.

The worst cases

Some rescues provide permanent homes to some dogs that simply cannot be re-homed for various reasons, and which would otherwise have to be euthanized. These are usually individuals that have passed

◄ Some dogs can be nervous with people and winning their confidence can prove to be a slow process. Such individuals are not a good choice for a home with children and may be best-suited to sharing a home with just one person who can devote the necessary time to settle them in properly.

through numerous homes previously and have been badly treated, making them extremely nervous around anyone taking care of them.

They may end up being kept in domestic-type set-ups at the rescue in what appear to be rooms, with a sofa for example where the dog may sleep for part of the day. This type of situation works because of the dedication of staff at rescue centres, who carrying on looking after the dogs there every day of the year.

Winning back the confidence of dogs that have been badly abused by people can be a challenging task. Some never fully recover their trust, even if the physical injuries that they may have acquired heal well over time. Rescue dogs in this category are probably the most difficult cases to deal with, but on the other hand, hard-won success in this area can be immensely rewarding.

It is probably fair to say that they are only suitable for a tiny percentage of would-be owners, who can afford such dogs the time and compassion that is required to help them recover from their previous ordeal. As a general rule, people living on their

own, who work part-time from home or are retired, and have extensive experience with dogs are likely to get the best results.

A vicious cycle

Dogs usually end up in this state because of on-going, unresolved issues in their lives. What can easily happen is that a dog starts to develop behavioural issues, such as soiling in the home or proving to be destructive, and its owner then fails

to take effective steps to remedy the situation. Ultimately, after much scolding and even physical abuse, the dog finds itself unwanted. It may at this stage simply be sold on to an unsuspecting purchaser at a bargain price. In unfamiliar surroundings, the dog's previous patterns of behaviour resurface, and so the cycle continues. Ultimately, the dog passes to a rescue centre, which may try to re-home it and if this attempt proves to be unsuccessful, then its future will start to look increasingly uncertain.

▼ Dogs that are unfortunate enough to be suffering serious signs of past injury and other handicaps, such as the loss of an eye, can be hard to rehome.

Accessing help for hard to re-home dogs

Just because a dog may not be well-disposed towards others of its kind, or is nervous with people, does not mean that it cannot develop into a loyal and loving pet. The key thing is to be aware of issues of this type at the outset. There is plenty of professional help available to at least ameliorate – if not totally overcome – the dog's behavioural issues.

Many larger rescue organizations have behaviourists on staff for dealing with such problems, and the likelihood is that this work will have started even before you acquire the dog. In other cases, what can happen is that the shelter has an arrangement with accredited behaviourists to assess dogs, and to work with those which have problems after they have been re-homed. Under these circumstances, the shelter usually pays the fees, but obviously, this comes out of their working budget, and you may therefore feel that you want to take

◄ *Most rescue centres will carry out an independent assessment of dogs that pass into their care, rather than just relying on the information that they receive, as this can be misleading. New arrivals tend not to be available for rehoming immediately partly for this reason.*

▼ *With suitable training, it is possible to overcome many behavioural issues, but this will require determination and dedication on your part.*

on this responsibility, by making an equivalent donation back to the organization.

On-going support can be critical in ensuring that a dog with previous behavioural issues settles well in a new home. Nevertheless, you will

inevitably need to be prepared to play your part, by working with your new pet to institute the recommended changes that will hopefully resolve the issue. In some cases, this may only be for a transitory period, although in others, you may need to work on the issues throughout the dog's life.

Health care support

A similar situation applies in the case of a dog's health. Although only the larger rescue organizations employ veterinary staff directly and may even have their own operating and recovery units in some rare cases, even small rescues will have a relationship with a local veterinary practice which oversees the wellbeing of their dogs.

Help will therefore be close at hand if you need it, and this is particularly significant for dogs that are suffering with ongoing medical conditions such as *diabetes mellitus*.

▲ *Nervousness is common in dogs that were not properly socialized as puppies or have been badly mistreated by their previous owner.*

▲ *Aggression towards other dogs is something that may require the dog to wear a muzzle when out walking.*

Regular monitoring and advice will be available, emphasizing the benefit of seeking a dog close to home in the first instance. If you live far away, the rescue may be willing to enter into an agreement with a veterinary practice closer to home and meet the costs of the dog's treatment.

Organize help

If you must go out at regular times for work, and your dog is nervous about being left alone, then you may need to utilize a dog-sitting service. This will help to prevent your home being damaged in your absence, if your pet suffers from separation anxiety, while you aim to overcome your pet's fear of being left alone.

You can track down those offering services of this kind in your area quite easily, but try to obtain recommendations, from friends, the rescue centre, or your veterinary practice as a starting point. It is also a good idea to let your dog meet the person concerned, to see how they bond – maybe with a trial session or two, before entering any regular, ongoing agreement.

What can work particularly well is if you can organize things so that the dog-sitter takes your pet for a walk when you are out. This has the benefit of helping to divert your dog's attention from your absence and means that it will be more likely to settle down and sleep on its return, potentially helping to break the separation anxiety of your pet as a result.

DAMAGE IN THE HOME

Any damage that arises will partly depend where in the home your dog has access, and this needs to be considered at the outset. It is possible to overcome the problem successfully with careful therapy training, but the impact will not be instant. You will need to be patient and redesign your home as far as possible to minimize any damage. Puppies too can prove to be destructive on occasions, notably when they are teething, but this is a temporary phase, and will pass before long.

When you take on a dog, therefore, check your home insurance policy. A few household policies these days provide cover for any serious damage in the home caused by your pet, and this can prove to be a useful and reassuring option just in case anything of major value is badly damaged, as it can then be repaired or replaced.

▶ *Learning as much about a dog's responses to people, other dogs and toys (as shown here) will give a useful insight into the best type of home for it, and how to resettle it successfully.*

Assessing your commitment

The sad truth is that some people who choose to take on a dog are not able to make the necessary commitment. It is often not just a question of the financial outlay, but that people take on a dog and fail to appreciate that it could quite easily live into its teens, and will need constant daily care. Careful consideration into what is required when taking on a rescue dog is vital.

Sometimes, the enthusiasm that was there initially, in terms of having a pet and bonding with it gradually falls away to the point that the dog becomes largely left to its own devices. It gets bored and becomes destructive, causing resentment and weakening the bond between dog and owner even further. This is why many dogs end up in rescues. There is a phrase that is often quoted by those who work in the rescue field, "there are no bad dogs, only bad owners", and fundamentally, this is the reality of the situation.

A long-term commitment
You therefore need to be brutally honest at the outset, to save yourself and other family members from disappointment, and more importantly, a rescue dog from becoming homeless again. Are you

▲ Having to go into residential care could mean that an elderly owner may be forced to give up their dog unexpectedly.

able to look after a pet now, given your individual situation, and looking ahead into the foreseeable future?

As mentioned, taking on a rescue dog can often prove to be even more

challenging than starting with a puppy, and the key thing that you need, particularly at first, is the time to get to know your new pet and start to build a bond between you. Planning is very important. It is not ideal if you start out with a new dog a month before heading off on an overseas holiday, so your dog will need to go back into kennels. Instead, wait to search for a dog until after your return. You will then be able to concentrate on building a bond and integrating your new companion into your household. It is very important to devote time specifically to your pet, particularly in the early stages, to win its confidence and trust.

Likely expenditure
It is important to consider the impact of looking after your pet on your household budget. Should you be uncertain of the costs involved and want to get a more accurate idea of

◄ Large dogs are more costly to keep, and this can strain a family's budget under difficult financial circumstances, forcing them to relinquish their pet.

▶ You must have plenty of free time to devote to your new canine companion and be prepared to provide plenty of reassurance, so that it can settle in quickly.

the figures, find a pet store online. Look at the prices of food and equipment, and then you can work out an appropriate budget, based on the size of dog that you are thinking of acquiring.

It is obvious that a large dog will have a bigger appetite than a smaller individual, and so will cost more to feed, but there are other less obvious costs that may become apparent. Grooming is a key example, because the terrier breeds for example traditionally need regular professional grooming to look their best, adding to the cost of ownership.

Rescue centres usually always ensure that their dogs are neutered, before allowing them to go to their 'forever home', and will usually have arranged your pet's vaccinations too, but you will be responsible for them going forwards. The range required will depend on where you live in the world, and whether you intend to travel far with your dog in due course.

▶ Dogs that pass into the care of rescue centres are normally neutered before being rehomed, to help prevent adding to the numbers of unwanted puppies. This can also make them easier to manage and should avoid health issues such as pyometra in bitches.

There will also be several one-off costs at the outset which need to be borne in mind. You may have to adapt your vehicle so that you can transport your dog safely, depending on its size. A carrying crate may work for a smaller individual, while a dog guard (depending on your vehicle) will be required for a bigger dog.

Time for socializing and training

Dogs are social animals and it is important to spend time with them, walking, playing, cuddling and generally making them feel wanted. To end up with a dog that is confident, loyal and friendly you need to commit time every day to bond with them, and above all be patient and allow them the time to settle in, learn new routines and what is expected of them.

If you are starting out with a puppy, you may well need to pay for training classes, typically from about six months onwards, although it may also be recommended to take your pet to puppy socialization courses before this stage as well. Your dog may also have certain behavioural issues that are best resolved with some targeted specialist training.

Assessing your lifestyle

The one thing that you must avoid above all else is creating a similar cycle that leads to dogs being handed into rescue organizations by their owners who cannot cope with them. How your new pet will impact on all the members of your family, your work and other pets in the house are all key things to consider. Even where you live can have a bearing on whether to commit to a rescue dog.

Lives are busy these days, and you need to be certain that you can integrate your dog easily into your domestic circumstances without it becoming a stressful experience for either party.

Work-dog balance

The first hurdle relates to your working routine – obviously, things ought to be much easier if you are retired, because you are likely to have more time to settle your dog into its new surroundings and develop a routine together. This is very important in helping to build the bond between you in the early days, particularly in the case of a dog that has been mistreated and is nervous.

It will be more difficult if you are commuting regularly to work, unless there is someone else at home to be with the dog. Problems can easily arise, particularly in the case of puppies or older individuals which are not effectively house-trained, even if your absence is quite short.

You may well come back to find that your home has been soiled in your absence, and although the occasional accident may not matter, this can soon develop into a repetitive problem which will be harder to overcome and may frequently be accompanied by destructive behaviour too. Even if you can take your dog to work, this will not be feasible until it is trained and confident around people, and so is unlikely to provide a solution.

In some situations, it may be better to seek out an older individual. If a dog of this type is then taken for a good walk before you leave home,

▲ *Dogs appreciate having a routine in their lives, and you must have free time to spend with your pet on a daily basis.*

there are less likely to be issues arising in your absence. The chances are that your dog will simply curl up and go to sleep until you return, but you do need to have set up this routine in advance. A dog that finds itself abandoned in surroundings on its own, with unfamiliar scents and noises will obviously not be relaxed and inclined to settle down.

Considerations around children

The presence of children in the home is something that rescues are very alert to, when considering the suitability of dogs for certain homes. In the first instance, some breeds,

◀ *Older dogs tend to be calmer than puppies, assuming they are used to living in a home environment.*

▶ *Choosing a suitable rescue dog for a home where young children live can be particularly difficult, and close supervision will be necessary.*

notably members of the toy group, which have been kept living closely alongside people over the course of centuries, are best suited for this purpose than those developed for guarding purposes, which can be less tolerant.

The age of the children is significant too, because if your children are toddlers, then a relatively large, boisterous dog can result in them being accidentally knocked over in the home. Your choice under these circumstances will therefore be more restricted and you may have to be more patient as a result. The background of the dog is important nevertheless, as an individual that

▼ *Your dog will require its own space in your home, and you will need to consider how best to accommodate it.*

has spent its entire life with an elderly person will probably not settle well into what can be a frenetic household alongside a couple of lively children.

In many cases, a cross-bred puppy may be a better choice, as it will grow up in the household and will not have had previous bad experiences, and so should not be unduly nervous, as well as being at a stage where it can be trained relatively easily.

If your children are approaching their teen years or are older, then things are more straightforward, but it is worth bearing in mind that dogs

HOW BIG WILL A PUPPY GROW?

It is not always easy to assess the likely adult size of a puppy if its ancestry is unknown. Domestic dogs alive today vary in size from a height of about 15cm (6in) as in the case of Chihuahua through to 91cm (36in) as typified by an Irish wolfhound. Yet the range of size in puppies is not so marked. Those of bigger breeds are relatively small at birth, and then grow more quickly in size than their smaller counterparts.

The same applies in the case of mongrel puppies too. There is one very clear indicator that you can use to give an insight into their likely adult size however, by looking at their feet. If these are proportionately large, then the puppies will grow into relatively big dogs.

◄ *Cats and dogs can become the best of friends, but it will be much easier if you can acquire a dog that has lived with a cat previously. They should then settle well together.*

can pick up on the high energy levels of children, so you will need space where it is possible for them to run around safely.

Living with a resident cat

It is worth bearing in mind that certain types of dogs are more likely to pursue cats than others. Ex-racing greyhounds, although gentle by nature, are often particularly difficult around cats, regarding a feline companion as the furred hare that they never managed to catch on the track but have not given up pursuing ever since. Sighthounds of this type are not a good choice for a household with a resident cat.

The same applies in the case of lurchers, which also frequently find their way into rescues. These are not a breed as such, but a distinctive type of hunting dog. Lurchers are bred from crosses between sighthounds and members of the pastoral group of breeds such as collies, or terriers. Some of these crosses can prove to be quite

complex, featuring greyhound, deerhound and Saluki crosses for example on the hound side, combined with Border collies and Bedlington terriers on the other.

Lurchers were originally bred – and are still used in some places even today – as poacher's dogs. They can display excellent pace, thanks to their sighthound ancestor, and possess the resourceful, intelligent nature of the sheepdog and terrier. Such dogs are used to working silently alongside their handler, and are very variable in appearance, as is to be anticipated with their highly mixed ancestry.

Members of this group do make excellent family pets in many cases however, proving affectionate and responsive companions, but it is important to realise that lurchers possess a keen hunting instinct. This in turn often gives them a desire to chase that is not in keeping with their otherwise friendly temperament.

Nevertheless, it is quite possible to keep a cat alongside a sighthound or

lurcher, but in this case, the chances of harmony will be very greatly enhanced by starting off with a puppy, rather than an older individual. This then means that the young dog grows up recognizing that the cat is part of the family and does not challenge its more dominant position within the existing hierarchy.

As a guide, small dogs are likely to be suitable companions where there are cats already in the home. This is not just a reflection of their background, but also because a cat will often turn and stare down a dog of this size if it starts to try to assert itself. This then ensures that harmony should prevail quite quickly, and the

▼ *Sighthounds and lurchers (as seen below) can be the most difficult to integrate into a home with a cat, because of their speed.*

APARTMENT LIFE

If you are living in an apartment, you may be barred from having a dog under the terms of your lease. However, as the benefits of pet-ownership have become better studied by scientists, so there are moves to prevent general bans on living with pets.

Being realistic, however, it will be particularly difficult to care for a dog if you live in a high-rise apartment block without access to a garden. Under these circumstances, there will probably be other pets that will be much easier to care for, such as guinea pigs, that can be kept indoors with no risk of upsetting near neighbours. It is worth remembering that the barking of small dogs tends not to be scaled down significantly, to reflect their size.

established order will not be challenged. Indeed, over time, dogs and cats can build up a strong bond together, even to the extent that a dog will protect its companion from other neighbourhood cats that may try to invade the garden.

Taking on more than one dog

On occasions, dogs that have lived in the same home for a long time and formed a very close bond can end up in a rescue centre and need to be re-homed together. Dogs in this

▶ Dogs that are used to each other will readily play together but introducing a second dog to your home will not be as straightforward.

situation can present a particular problem when it comes to finding them a forever home, partly because of the increased costs and space that is required to look two dogs adequately.

It is often assumed that keeping two dogs together means that they will occupy each other, making their care more straightforward. But the reality is that it is much harder to train them effectively, as you need to

▲ In cases where two dogs have grown up together, it will usually help to settle them into a new home more easily if they are not separated.

maintain their concentration in both cases. Simply allowing them to interact will make it harder to communicate effectively, and so the chances are that they may not be as well-trained as might have been hoped.

CHAPTER TWO

FINDING YOUR IDEAL COMPANION

Having taken the decision to look for your forever canine companion, it is only natural that you will be keen to find this dog and have it join your household as soon as possible. But it is important to be realistic and appreciate that this may not be a quick process, and that it may be partly influenced by the time of year.

Rescue organizations will not generally re-home dogs over the Christmas period for example, because of the almost inevitable disturbances in people's lives at this time. This makes it very difficult to establish a routine in the first instance, and there are other potential difficulties, in terms of chocolate and other foods that a new dog could steal, which would make it ill.

The ideal time of year to obtain a new dog – and particularly a puppy – will be in the spring, as it will be much easier, with the weather improving, to house-train your pet. The weather will also be better to spend time outdoors playing with your pet, helping to establish a close bond between you. Then, if you want to go away later in the year on holiday, your pet should have mastered the basics of training, and may be able to come with you, depending on where you are going.

Bear in mind too that even when you locate your dream companion, you will still need to be patient. You will probably have to make several visits to the rescue centre, so you and the dog will be able to start to form a bond. In addition, it will be necessary to arrange an assessor's visit, ensuring all is well for your chosen dog to join you permanently.

◄ *There are several factors that will influence how quickly your new companion can join you, and you may well need to be patient.*

Beginning the search

Having decided to provide a forever home for a rescue dog it is time to start loooking. There are a few ways in which you can achieve this, with an internet search often proving to be the best starting point. Typing a term such as 'dog re-homing and adoption' and your location into a search engine should return a variety of results, listing organizations near you.

The benefits of approaching a dog rescue centre will be that they are experienced in what they do, and will be able to advise on the suitability of a dog for your situation. Staff will also be on hand for advice at any stage in the process, even after you have taken your pet home.

Which rescue centre?

There are several different types of dog rescue set-ups. Firstly, some are operated by national organizations, working through a series of local branches, whereas others are strictly local, being run largely by volunteers.

▼ Dogs may often be more nervous than normal when meeting you in a rescue centre. Crouching down at first can be less intimidating for them under these circumstances.

▲ It can be very distressing to see dogs in rescue centres needing homes, but equally, it is vital for both you and the dog that you make the right choice. The staff there can help to guide you.

While most homing centres have a mixed range of dogs, often with a high percentage of individuals of indeterminate parentage, there are also some specialist breed rescues too. These tend to be structured slightly differently, being operated by members of breed societies who keep such dogs themselves.

Breed rescues typically foster dogs that need new homes, rather than accommodating them in kennels. This is often the best place to start if you are in search of a particular type of pooch, although you may discover some pure-bred dogs amongst those in general rescue centres. This is especially true of popular breeds such Staffordshire bull terriers. You are also likely to find that there is a long waiting list at breed rescues, as they have relatively few dogs available for re-homing.

▶ *It may be easier in some cases than others to determine the likely ancestry of a particular dog. In this case, the dog on the left is clearly of spitz type, with a broad head and pricked ears.*

If you are having difficulty in tracking down a particular breed rescue, it can be worthwhile contacting the national kennel club, which oversees the registration of dogs and breeders. They generally have this information available or can direct you to someone involved with the breed who might be able to help.

Many dog re-homing websites not only have photographs and videos of the dogs that are available, but also background information about the individuals too. Bear in mind that this can only be a guide, although the details here will usually give you some insights into the likely age, temperament, and the level of training an individual has received. Other information, such as how a particular dog behaves around other dogs and cats may also be included.

Building a picture

From many points of view, when you are looking to re-home a rescue dog, and may not have that much

▶ *It will take time to build up a close bond with a rescue dog, especially one that has been mistreated in the past, but you should soon be able to tell if there is a rapport between you when you meet, based on the dog's reactions to you.*

experience of dog-ownership, it will be better to focus your search on dogs that have a reasonably well-defined history and are used to living in domestic surroundings. When you start searching on the internet, you are likely to find details about a dog's past, and why it has unfortunately ended up in care. The individual listing will usually give some indication into its temperament, and details about its previous life, including information about whether it was living with another dog perhaps, or indeed a cat.

Dogs in this category will be used to domestic surroundings, having previously been used to some degree of human company, rather than living on the streets. They may be

well-trained, including being clean indoors, and will settle back into home life with minimal difficulty.

The staff at the rescue centre will be able to give you some idea about the level of a dog's training, and obviously, if you are exercising the dog yourself, as part of building a bond together, you will be able to determine this for yourself.

In the case of dogs whose previous owners have died, it may be harder to gain insight into whether they have been recently vaccinated for example, and if they have been spayed (neutered) in the case of bitches, where this change is not very evident once the surgical incision heals properly.

It will obviously be helpful if the dog's health records are available, but if not, then a veterinary examination should be able to determine whether this surgery has been carried out or not, to avoid adding the toll of unwanted puppies in the world. With male dogs that have been castrated however, the situation will be very clear. Most rescues will only re-home neutered dogs in any case, and will arrange for appropriate surgery to be carried out beforehand if necessary.

Obtaining a dog from another country

If you travel a lot, the chances are that you will spot stray dogs on the street, or alternatively, you might find overseas dog rescues on the internet. Bringing a dog from abroad is much easier than it used to be but there are still several factors to take into account. Is the dog free to travel? Will it have to go into quarantine? What paperwork needs to be completed? These are all important considerations.

If you are staying in an area and come across a stray dog, you may start to build up a bond by feeding it. This then raises the question of what you should do when you are heading home. In some cases, you may be drawn towards thinking about bringing the dog back with you. But is this feasible – or even desirable?

Much depends on your situation, and primarily, that of the dog in question. In many parts of the world, dogs are allowed to roam freely, and it may well be that your perceived stray does in fact have a home nearby. It has learnt to come and seek food where you are staying, because of the generous nature of visitors at the property, before wandering back to its permanent home.

Trying to take this dog back home with you could cause serious complications. It is vital to determine that any dog in this type of situation is truly homeless and living on the streets, because otherwise, dog-napping could have severe consequences – even resulting in a charge of theft! It is worthwhile not just checking with people in the area, but also asking at the police station.

On the move

The ease – and therefore the cost – of taking a stray dog back home with you will depend partly on where you are living, relative to where you found the dog. Within Europe, it is currently much easier to travel with dogs from one country to another, but almost inevitably, the necessary requirements mean that you will have to go home and make suitable arrangements, rather than travelling back immediately with your new companion. You will therefore need to find someone who can arrange to look after the dog during this period for you. It may be a friend in the area, or boarding kennels.

There is now quite a widely recognized travel scheme for dogs, applying not just within the European Union and to the UK, but extending further afield as well, encompassing the USA, Mexico and several Caribbean islands, Australia, and Japan, for example. With the correct paperwork, dogs can typically travel between these countries without having to be quarantined, which used to be the only option in the past, but always check the current regulations carefully in advance.

In some cases, the dog will have to be placed in quarantine. This can be costly, and although there are people taking care of dogs in quarantine kennels, it does mean that they will be rather isolated and deprived of human company throughout this period, which typically lasts about four months.

Identification

Whenever a dog is travelling internationally, it is vital to make sure that it is identifiable. Today, this is achieved by means of a microchip implant. Measuring about the size of a grain of rice, this must be placed under the skin of the neck, by adopting a similar technique to giving an injection.

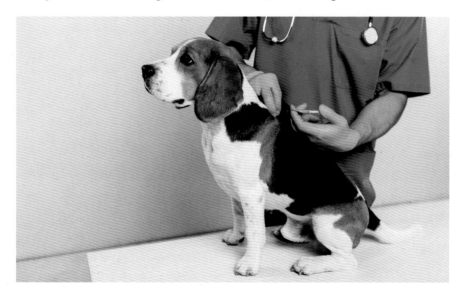

◄ *Moving dogs from one country to another can be challenging, in terms of following the health and shipping rules, but there are companies specializing in this area.*

◄ *Even though most dogs are unused to travelling in a container by air, they generally do not become upset.*

► *Rules apply to the design of containers used to carry dogs by air, and appropriate labelling is also essential.*

The microchip will contain a unique code number, and this is read by passing a special reader over the injection site, which in turn activates the chip. The number shows up as a digital display on the reader's screen. As a result, it is then possible to check this number against that logged on the dog's official health and travel documents, confirming that everything is in order.

Microchipping also ensures that your dog can be listed on a database, so that if it strays or is stolen and subsequently recovered in either case, you can be notified and there can be no dispute over its identity. In some areas of the world, all dogs must now be micro-chipped by law.

Health controls

A key aspect of the paperwork is to ensure that your dog is effectively vaccinated against rabies. This killer viral disease, for which there is no cure, can affect people as well, and so a rabid dog is exceedingly dangerous. The vaccine required needs to be either an inactivated or recombinant vaccine, approved for use in the country concerned, to comply with the regulations. Only dogs that are at least 12 weeks of age can be vaccinated, because under this age, the vaccine may fail

to work effectively (the puppies may have received some temporary immunity against the rabies virus from their mother).

As far as entry to Great Britain is concerned, you will then need to wait three weeks before you can bring your dog back to its new home. Things are more complicated in the case of other countries that are excluded from the travel scheme because they are considered to be higher risk. Following its rabies vaccination, your pet will then need a blood test more than 30 days later, which must be carried out in an approved laboratory, to ensure your dog's vaccination was successful. It is then a matter of waiting a further three months before your dog can return home with you, so this process will take a total of four months.

In either case, between one and five days before you depart, you will need to visit the vet again. On this occasion, your dog must be treated for tapeworm, using a recognized drug known to be effective against the *Echinococcus multilocularis* tapeworm. This is another zoonosis – a disease that can be spread between animals and people – and you must have the appropriate official certification that the treatment has been administered.

Returning home

When booking to return with your dog, it is important to remember that there may be only certain routes that you can take to enter your home country when bringing your pet with you. This applies in the case of air and seaports, as well as rail routes. You may be able to return as a foot passenger on a boat though, depending on the carrier – these too are specified.

As always, it is very important to ensure that you adhere to the latest rules, because these can be subject to change. Shipping container regulations must also be followed, should your dog be travelling by air. If you feel rather overwhelmed by all this, there are specialist animal shipping companies that will undertake all the necessary arrangements for you and will liaise with the carrier and custom officials.

However you decide to proceed, always plan from the outset, and give yourself adequate time to get everything properly organized. Above all, remember that bringing a dog back from abroad will be a time-consuming procedure, quite apart from being relatively costly, and is definitely not something that should be undertaken without adequate thought in advance.

Contacting the rescue centre

The way in which rescue organizations are structured does affect the way that they deal with enquiries. Their website will be a good starting point by which to make contact, including an email address, although in the case of breed rescues staffed entirely by volunteers, you may need to get in touch by phone as they may not have a website.

◄ There are different types of rescue organizations seeking homes for dogs, operating in various ways.

as well as your previous experience (if any) of dog-ownership. This will then help staff firstly to ensure that the dog that you have chosen will be suitable for your lifestyle, saving you from potential disappointment later. The information will also assist them to find alternative possibilities for you, if necessary, which may represent better options.

The type of background information that is useful is the rough size of your home and garden, as well as whether you have children, and what their ages are, noting also if you already have a dog or indeed other pets. The amount of time that you are at home can be helpful too,

Some of the larger organizations have a national presence, so it makes sense to track down the centre nearest to you. This is a good point to start looking, and then expand out from here to centres further afield. Bear in mind that you will almost certainly need to make several trips to the centre to see a dog that appeals to you, so that distance can be significant. Also, if you subsequently need to have any behavioural support for your new companion, it will be much easier if this is available in your vicinity, so choosing a rescue centre close to home can have advantages.

Starting off
Read the advice on the rescue centre's website about getting in touch. Some prefer to be contacted by email rather than by phone. It is always better to arrange a visit, so that someone should be available to help you. Bear in mind that in the case of larger centres that are open to the public, if you simply turn up unannounced, you may have to wait to be seen. There is also the risk, especially if you are travelling any distance, that your chosen dog may already just have found its forever home or might have gone out for a walk, meaning that you have had a wasted journey.

Providing background information
In the first instance, don't just say that you are interested in a specific dog on the organization's website and would like to see it. Instead, it will be helpful if you provide some information about yourself and any other members of your household,

▼ Be prepared to be patient when in search of a canine companion that will fit your lifestyle.

◄ *You are likely to encounter dogs of various sizes and ages in rescues. There can be advantages to choosing an older dog rather than a puppy.*

ARRANGING A VISIT

Once you hear back from the rescue centre, the next step – assuming they have dogs that might be suitable for you – will be to arrange a visit. If possible, it may be better to go on a weekday, rather than at the weekend when most larger centres are likely to be busier with visitors. This means that a member of staff may be able to spend more time with you, which can be especially helpful if you have not had a dog before, as it means you can ask any questions that come to mind.

Be prepared for the fact that it is usually very different meeting a dog for the first time whose photograph you have previously only seen online. Some re-homing centres are now posting videos as well, to give a better overall idea of the dogs in their care that are available for re-homing. These can help to give an indication of the dog's size.

based on what you do, plus a brief insight as to why you think that your choice of dog would be well-suited to your lifestyle.

You may also want to include any specific details about your hobbies. As an example, if you regularly go mountain biking, and the dog that appeals to you will benefit from having plenty of exercise, then explain you are looking for a sporting companion who could join you on your regular trips out, after a period of suitable training.

In all cases, having a checklist will assist you in making a choice. There are several factors to bear in mind. If you are searching for a puppy, and are not wanting to have an older dog, this is something that needs to be documented. The coat type is significant, and of course, the size of dog. Training considerations may also influence your decision.

▼ *It is important to get to know a dog and discover how it bonds with you in the first instance.*

Questions to ask

When visiting the rescue centre try to find out as much information as you can about your potential pet. There are the basic questions, like how much is it eating, and how much exercise does it require, along with questions about its background. These may be trickier for staff to answer, partly because of confidentiality, but also because depending on the dog's history, little may be known about its past.

It is important that you feel confident that you will be able to look after your chosen dog and understand its needs more generally. It is always worth asking for any behavioural quirks that the staff may have noted. This type of knowledge can enable you to steer away from trouble in the future. The rule must always be to 'expect the unexpected', especially in the early stages when you are getting to know your new companion, as it may display previously unrecognized patterns of behaviour which link back to its previous experiences.

A typical 'real life' example involved a beagle which was regularly left alone for extremely long periods, so that it started soiling in the home, and was then badly beaten by its owner when she came home. Luckily, the dog was rescued and rehomed. After all the trauma that she had experienced, this beagle proved to be

▲ Rescue centres will be aware of any basic health issues surrounding a particular dog you are interested in taking home, such as dental problems.

▼ Unexpected triggers from your dog's past may surface unexpectedly, notably with those that have previously been mistreated.

remarkably well-adjusted to life, still possessing the very positive and bouncy demeanour that is such a characteristic feature of this breed.

All went well, until unexpectedly, on a rainy day, when walking along a pavement close to her home on a route that she knew well, the dog's demeanour changed dramatically. She refused to walk on, and pulled back, crouching down on the ground in a very evident state of distress as a passer-by approached. Only once the person had disappeared into the distance did the possible reason for this dramatic, extreme and unparalleled change in the dog's behaviour emerge.

It had to have been the bright colour of the coat of the woman who had walking past her in the street. With hindsight, although it was impossible to be certain, it is likely that the beagle's previous owner had probably worn a coat of

▲ *Dogs in rescue centres can vary from those that are very well trained through to those that have received no training at all.*

the same colour, which she had not taken off when she came home and started to punish the beagle on her return. The dog had therefore become conditioned to the sight of a similar coat and being beaten.

This example emphasizes the fact that not all aspects of a dog's past will be known to staff, and you do need to be aware that there can be triggers that may come up in the future. It is therefore important to remain alert and observant with your new pet going forwards, rather than assuming you have the full picture.

Appreciating the issues

Where there are known behavioural issues with a dog however, then the staff will be very happy to discuss these, explain them and outline what support is available to address the situation. In most cases, with a patient, caring owner and the requisite professional support, problems of this type can often be overcome, or at least ameliorated to a significant extent so they do not prove to be of major concern.

The same applies in the case of known health issues. The staff will be very willing to discuss these, and if, for example, you are nervous about injecting your dog regularly with insulin to control its diabetes, then they will show you how this is carried out and may highlight how to practice with an orange.

The matter of training

Training is another area that needs to be discussed. While some dogs in a general rescue's care will have been well-trained in the past, there will inevitably also be not just young puppies, but also older dogs that

▼ *Dogs with a hound ancestry – both sighthounds and scenthounds – are the most difficult in terms of basic recall training.*

▲ *Certain types of dogs such as gundogs and those with a herding ancestry are likely to be easier to train than others.*

have never been trained. This applies particularly in the case of street dogs which have previously spent their lives roaming around cities, feeding on scraps and handouts.

One of the significant aspects of going to visit a dog in a rescue is that you can gain a much clearer insight into how much basic training it has mastered. If you are drawn to an older dog that has never been trained, then this will represent a significant challenge going forwards. Puppies instinctively learn faster than an older individual, but with patience and the necessary help to iron out issues that crop up, it is possible to train an older dog successfully.

Bear in mind that certain dogs, such as those with a retriever or spaniel ancestry for example, whose ancestors were bred to work closely on a one-to-one basis with people, are likely to be more responsive and learn faster. In contrast, hound-type dogs are a much harder proposition, in terms of training, as they possess a naturally more free-spirited nature, which they won't be afraid to reveal!

The first meeting

No matter how good the care that a dog receives in a rescue, it will not be totally relaxed in the same way that it would be at home, when it comes to meeting visitors to the rescue centre. The way that dogs react to encountering strangers varies significantly, being influenced in part by the dog's past experiences. A careful, steady approach will be necessary on your first meeting.

Some dogs tend to be naturally friendlier than others. This is likely to reflect both their ancestry and their experience of life. Individuals descended from breeds which have a protective personality, typically guard dogs, are instinctively likely to be more withdrawn, but equally any dog that is not used to human company or has been mistreated will require time and understanding to get its confidence back. The staff will probably have an idea as to how the dog will react in any case and will do their best to ensure that it is a positive experience for all concerned. Rest assured, however, that if the encounter does not go well, this will not be a personal reflection on you.

▼ *After the initial period of sniffing, then it is usually fine to start stroking the dog gently and start to build up a bond between you.*

First impressions

There will probably be a quiet area within the rescue organization's premises where you can meet your chosen dog, or you might even go out together with the staff member for a short walk. You will be able to gain some insight into the dog's demeanour when you first see it. If the dog is feeling confident, then it will be lively, interacting with the

◄ *Always give a rescue dog space when you first meet. Try to be relaxed – even though you will inevitably be excited!*

handler, although not necessarily doing what it is told. On the other hand, a nervous dog will tend to pull back, hiding behind its handler and displaying little enthusiasm for being out of its kennel.

It is important to appreciate that the way in which you react can have a definite impact on the dog's behaviour too. It is always a good idea to crouch or bend down, so you are more on the dog's eye level than towering over it. This applies particularly in the case of a dog that has been mistreated in some way, as it may then cower away, having become accustomed in the past to being hit by someone standing over it. Avoid any sudden movements as well, especially with your arms, that could upset the dog and cause it to pull back.

In your enthusiasm, do not rush to touch the dog. Let it focus on you, and gently offer it your hand to sniff, so that it can pick up your scent. As a species, we are much more visually orientated than dogs, relying almost entirely on our eyesight, whereas scent is of increased significance to dogs. Bearing this in mind, it may be better not to wear any aftershave or scent just in case this triggers unpleasant past memories of the dog's former life, which could be upsetting for it.

◄ It will be essential to allow a rescue dog to get to know you over the course of several visits, helping your new pet to settle in with you in due course when you ultimately head home together.

Making progress

Assuming the dog reacts favourably after your initial encounter, you can then gently move your hand round and stroke the back of its head. Talk quietly to the dog throughout, using its name which it will recognize. Don't raise your voice, even though you may be excited, as the dog may take this as a threat, based on its previous experiences.

Even if you have gone to visit with another member of your family, it is probably better if you both introduce yourselves separately on the first occasion. Otherwise, the dog could feel crowded by being confronted by two people, making it nervous.

After the initial introductions, you may opt to go out for a walk together. Not only does this give you an opportunity to bond, but it also allows you to gain an insight into how responsive the dog is, in terms of walking on the leash, and whether it is inclined to pull ahead. When you are out together, carry on talking to the dog, using its name. This is especially important if it is nervous, as can apply in the case of dogs that have spent their lives living in kennels, or those that have been shut up in homes and rarely taken out.

What next?

By the end of this initial introduction, you will have got to know your chosen dog much better, from being just a photograph and possibly a video on screen through to seeing it as a potential companion with its own, very distinctive personality. This is not to say that you then immediately must take a decision as to whether this particular individual is the dog to join your household. Indeed, there will be no pressure to do so from the staff. They appreciate that it is a big step and commitment, and it is easy to get swept along in the emotion of the moment.

It doesn't reflect any hesitancy or reluctance on your part if you say that you want to think about it further and come back to see the dog again. In that way, you can be sure that you are making the right choice. What usually happens is that the dog will be reserved for you, and you can make several trips back to the centre, building up a bond between you.

► Taking the rescue dog out for a walk away from the centre is a good way of getting acquainted. You can also discover how well the dog walks on the leash – it may persistently pull, for example, which is something that you will need to work on, as this can be dangerous if the dog steps out into the road ahead of you when a car is coming towards you.

The assessor's visit

There are a lot of myths and even sometimes concern attached to this aspect of the re-homing process. The assessor's visit is a standard practice for most rescues and does not reflect personally on you or your individual domestic arrangements. It is procedure, with the aim of hopefully ensuring that the dog will be able to settle quickly with you in what will become its forever home.

All pet adoption agencies generally send out an assessor in advance to check a new home for one of their dogs. The larger bodies operating in this area may employ staff members, part of whose duties are to go out and visit those wanting to re-home dogs, whereas smaller organizations rely on volunteers to undertake this task. This stage in the re-homing of a rescue dog should not be seen as worrying or stressful, but simply part of the process. There is no need to get alarmed in any way, or to undertake any special preparation.

How it works

In most cases, an appointment is made at a convenient time for the assessor to call, and then it will be a matter of showing the assessor

▲ *Dogs vary in their suitability for different types of home and matching your choice with your home is vital.*

around the rooms in your home where the dog will have access and walking round the garden together as well. Despite all your attempts to make the environment as safe as possible, there may still be some things that need doing, to keep your pet safe, which you have overlooked. The assessor can help you to settle your dog into your home, by having the opportunity to highlight any potential pitfalls that may have escaped your attention, like a gap under a gate that the dog could slip beneath in an unguarded moment. The assessor will also be able to talk through the rescue centre's policies

on formal adoption and what will happen next.

It also gives the opportunity to have a detailed discussion about the specific care of your chosen dog, with someone who is well-versed in dog care and specifically, the challenges that owning a rescue dog can throw up, as well as highlighting the rewards. It obviously helps to read up on the care and training of a dog in advance, but equally, you will not be subjected to an oral examination in the subject!

Think in advance about any questions that you may have and write them down as they come to mind so that you don't forget to ask them. The assessor's visit should prove to be a positive experience, with the sole aim of ultimately helping your dog to settle into its new home with you.

▼ *After an initial period of sniffing, it is usually fine to start stroking the dog gently to start building up a bond.*

► *Having an experienced dog person checking your garden for safety can be advantageous, allowing you to make any changes before your new companion joins you. This may extend to your choice of plants.*

Cleanliness

The assessor may bring the dog to meet you on the visit, so it has an opportunity to explore its new home. One thing that may be worth doing, if you had a dog previously, is to clean the floors, including the carpets, as thoroughly as possible. This is especially important if you had an elderly dog that became incontinent towards the end of its life.

Even if you cleared up after accidents in the home very thoroughly, it is likely that the newcomer will still be able to detect its scent. The human nose only contains about five million specialist olfactory cells, whereas dogs, having around 300 million cells, possess vastly superior scenting skills. As a result, the problem that can arise is that the new dog decides to eliminate the scent of its predecessor and starts to urinate again in these same areas.

Unfortunately, the use of an ordinary household cleaner will probably not be sufficient to eliminate the scent effectively, and so the problem will continue. It will be much better to obtain one of the specialist products sold through pet stores that are designed to be effective at eliminating odours of this type.

An experienced eye

If there are any suggestions that the assessor recommends, then obviously, these should be carried out if possible. There can be specific 'hidden' issues that only an experienced eye may pick up, based partly on the size and athleticism of the dog concerned. As an example, many people who like dogs also appreciate wildlife, and are keen to encourage wild birds for example, by setting up a feeding station in their garden.

Although dogs won't generally eat seed, the majority love the fat balls made of suet that are hung off bird tables or off tree branches. If your chosen companion is a large dog that could jump up and reach the fat ball, then this must be moved – possibly being hung instead on the front of your property out of your dog's reach. Otherwise, your dog could easily suffer serious diarrhoea after eating the fat ball.

Finally...

While most re-homing applications are approved, if you are turned down for the dog of your choice by the rescue centre at any stage in the process, this is not something to take personally. It is a reflection on your lifestyle, relative to the needs of the dog, which are paramount for the rescue centre. Be patient and don't give up hope, as it may well be that there is another dog in need of a forever home that would fit in much better with your lifestyle.

▼ *There could be things that you can do to help a dog to settle with you, which an assessor may be able to identify.*

Getting to know your rescue dog

Being aware and having a keen sense of anticipation are important aspects when it comes to keeping a dog, especially a rescued individual, and it helps to develop these skills from the outset. As you begin to get to know a dog, therefore, watch its reactions when it is out with you, and you can build up a picture of its level of confidence, based on its body language.

◄ *Some dogs are much better-trained than others. This is something that you need to know right at the outset.*

Playing games

Many rescue centres have a secure paddock or similar area where it is possible to allow a dog off the leash so that it can run around in safety. Here you will be able to gain further insight into a dog's behaviour, and how responsive it is, in terms of playing games for example, chasing after a ball or similar toy, and bringing it back to you. Bear in mind that some dogs are instinctively more playful than others, with those having a retriever breed ancestry being an example of a dog that is normally very keen to get involved with ball games.

There will also often be cases where a dog will never have played with toys before and may only be learning to chase after a ball. They can learn remarkably quickly though, given positive encouragement, and

Obtaining as much information as you can from the staff at the rescue centre from the outset is very valuable. They will be more than willing to share their findings with you, regarding dogs that appeal to you, so that you go into the re-homing project with your eyes open. Bear in mind that each dog's experiences will nevertheless be unique, and not every aspect of an individual's pattern of behaviour will necessarily have emerged in its interactions with staff.

It is also important to consider how the dog bonds with you. Looking after a dog is a very personal relationship. Undeniably, certain dogs strike up a closer relationship with some people than others, as they

seem to prefer them, for reasons that are unclear. There can also be situations where a young puppy was looked after mainly by one member of the household, and so instinctively feels drawn to a person of that gender in future.

◄ *Young rescue puppies will need training, just like any young dog. There are special classes that you can take your new companion to, working on the lessons at home as well. This should ensure that you have a well-trained dog in due course.*

▶ *It is important to determine if a rescue dog agrees with other individuals, when out for a walk. Bear in mind that balls can serve as a flashpoint for disagreements.*

pick up on what is required by watching other dogs too. The fact that a dog apparently has little interest in playing with a ball is therefore not a reflection on you, nor any cause for concern in the longer term. Indeed, older arthritic dogs may not be able to play in this way to any significant extent anyway.

Going for a walk

When you go out from the rescue centre with the dog, note how it reacts. Most dogs are keen to go out exploring for a walk, but some individuals may be nervous and seek

▼ *Do not allow your dog to pull ahead when you are out together. It will be harder to control otherwise, and the risk of conflict is increased if another dog comes bounding up when yours is restrained on a leash.*

to hang back, almost appearing reluctant to leave the confines of the rescue centre. Such behaviour can often be indicative of a dog that has spent much of its life confined in a small area, or may arise from being kept confined largely indoors in a home, with this reaction effectively resembling a form of agoraphobia.

There are also many things in the modern world that can be scary if you are not used to them, and this applies to dogs just as it does to humans. Note how the dog walks on the lead. Is it keen to go ahead of you, keeping its head up and

appearing confident? This is clearly a good sign, but beware if it starts to hold back, keeping its tail down and reaching the stage where it actively pulls back, because this is typically a nervous response. The dog is clearly not happy walking in that direction or in that area.

It is worth noting any change in the landscape at this point. Are you walking from open ground to a pavement perhaps, where the noise and proximity of passing traffic could be upsetting the dog? Always take care to ensure that it cannot pull out into the road at any stage. There is always a risk if there is another dog coming the opposite way down the pavement that a more nervous individual may attempt to pull away and step into the road.

As you gain personal experience of your dog's behaviour, so you can hopefully start to anticipate its reactions. There is always likely to be a potential flashpoint if a dog running free comes running up to another individual that is on a leash, and your dog may react badly when being confronted in this way. If your dog is known not to get on well with others, then it will be safest to take it out wearing a muzzle.

What dogs tell you

Dogs rely to a significant extent on their body language for communication purposes. The purpose behind the dog's body language is to indicate a mood or intention, and to do so in such a way that, in the case of what could otherwise become an aggressive encounter, the body language alone is enough to avoid a dangerous dispute occurring.

Domestic dogs have inherited many of the body language traits displayed by wolves, although changes in their anatomy have restricted their ability to express themselves so clearly. The positioning of the ears and tail in particular provide very important clues to a dog's mood, but bear in mind that not all breeds have the same degree of flexibility in their ears, which allows them to alter their posture easily.

Reading the signs

A nervous dog will crouch down close to the ground, holding its ears back against the head. Its tail will be held down between its hind legs. At the same time, its mouth will be open, and it will be growling. This serves as a warning. If you approach a dog more closely under these

▼ This individual is uncertain but is not backing down. Its hackles are raised, and it is showing its teeth.

circumstances, then the dog is likely to snap at you and look to run off if it can escape.

In contrast, a dog that is actively challenging you will display a very much more confident demeanour. It will be standing up, with its tail raised and its ears drawn forward and held erect. The hackles – the hair on the back of the neck – will be raised as well, serving to provide a means of making the dog look bigger and more intimidating.

It is likely to be barking loudly and repeatedly, as well as drawing back its lips to reveal its teeth. Dogs acting in this way are being very assertive and may well lunge and bite without any further provocation if you do not back away. Certain breeds, notably those developed as guardians, such as Rottweilers, tend to have more assertive personalities than others, and with their sharp teeth and strong jaws, dogs can inflict serious injury if they do attack.

However, under normal circumstances, a dog that is relaxed will approach with its tail up and wagging in a relatively slow, rhythmic way, with no sign of its hackles raised, and not growling at all. Here again though, as in the case of the ears, there are anatomical variations between different breeds which may affect this means of communication. For example, with the so-called spitz breeds from northern areas, the tail is relatively short and inflexible, naturally curling forward over the back.

A dog that is uncertain will hang back, holding its head down slightly, often keeping one of its front paws up, at least for periods of time. It may shift its position, without moving very far at all, as well as licking its lips rather nervously too.

▼ The dog seen here is frightened, as reflected by its posture – crouching down with its mouth open and growling at the same time.

◄ These two terriers are playing happily together. There is no sign of their hackles (the fur in the neck region) being raised to make them appear more intimidating.

ball or similar toy for you to throw, as a way of starting a game, lying down on its forelegs. At this stage, if it feels that it is still being ignored, your dog may start barking excitedly and repeatedly to attract your attention and bounce up before adopting the play bow posture again.

Once your dog starts reacting in this way towards you, it indicates that you are well on the way to having a trusting companion. Remember it is not just with you and people in your immediate circle, however, where your dog's body language can be significant. These indicators also apply when you are out walking, both when your dog meets people that it hasn't met before, as well as during encounters with other dogs.

If the dog starts to walk away, it is likely to do so with its tail hung low, between its legs. It will watch your movements and reactions very closely, while being careful not to stare directly at you as this action, in canine terms, is seen as a challenge.

In the case of rescue dogs that have had a bad start in life, their reactions can sometimes be more

extreme. For example, a dog that is particularly submissive may roll over on to the ground, lying on its back and sometimes urinating a little when in this position.

Keen to play

In contrast, a good sign which is seen frequently in young dogs particularly is the so-called 'play bow', which you are likely to see when you are interacting together, or when the dog wants to get your attention. Your pet will often bring a

▼ This dog is indicating its readiness to play, with its front legs extended flat on the ground and its hindquarters raised.

▼ After a period of exercise, a dog will soon learn to sit with you and relax, allowing you to reinforce the bond between you.

Safeguarding your home and garden

It is very important that when you bring your dog home, it will be coming back to live in a secure, safe environment. You will need to set time aside to go around your home and garden, checking if there is anything that needs to be done to prepare for your pet's arrival. This can only be done effectively once you have decided on the type, and more importantly perhaps, the size of dog that is coming home.

To avoid any potential breakages and the domestic disputes that may follow, take action before your dog arrives at your home.

Indoor precautions

Puppies that are teething around four to six months of age are likely to be most destructive in the home, and if you have any valued items of furniture that could end up being gnawed in a quiet moment, then it is a good idea to move them elsewhere before any damage can result.

Equally, if you have any rugs that are valuable, these too should be transferred elsewhere, as not only might they be chewed, but they could also be soiled with a puppy or indeed an older dog that is not house-trained. It is almost inevitable there will be some accidents indoors, even with the best-managed scenarios, so try to adapt things so that you can clean up easily

▲ *Special gates can be fitted in areas of your home to exclude dogs – but larger individuals may jump over them!*

afterwards. The kitchen is frequently recommended as a sleeping area for this reason, as the flooring here is often a hard surface, which can be mopped over and disinfected easily.

If the plan is to get a relatively large dog, then it is also a good idea to move any breakable ornaments off low shelves or tables, to protect them from being knocked over or broken. Bigger dogs can easily damage fragile items with their exuberant tail movements.

A particular danger in the home can be electrical cabling, as some dogs will chew this, clearly unaware that this could easily turn out to be life-threatening for them. The risk is greatest with puppies, but older dogs too may sometimes behave in this fashion. Before you bring a dog of any age into your household, it is a good idea to check if there is any loose cabling that could be put in a conduit and attached to the wall.

It is also a good idea to aim to keep electrical flexes attached to lamps and other electrical equipment off the floor as far as possible, making sure they will be out of your

▼ *Accidents happen. Develop a routine with a young dog, placing it outside every two hours or so.*

▼ *Trailing flexes are especially dangerous with puppies around. They may chew them or knock over the item above.*

▼ *Dogs can stand on their hind legs to reach edible items on a worktop or table, potentially breaking the container too.*

◄ *Do not underestimate how well an athletically built dog can jump, with those having long legs being most talented.*

dog's reach. Get into the habit of switching off this type of equipment at the wall socket when you are not present. This then guards against your dog being electrocuted should it be able to pick up the cabling and start chewing on it at any stage.

Outdoor precautions

While many dogs are happy simply to explore the garden, there are some which prove to be keen escape artists. These are usually young, fairly athletic individuals. They may detect the scent of food nearby, such as a neighbour having a barbecue, and seek a way to join the party.

Unneutered male dogs are particularly enthusiastic about leaving the garden when it comes to heading off in search of a nearby bitch in heat. This is another reason why neutering is important. Otherwise, as the time for mating approaches, so a female dog will release pheromones, which are chemical molecules that are wafted on air currents, and can be detected by males in the area, allowing them to track her down.

As most homes are adjacent to roads, it is very important to make sure that your garden is escape-proof as far as possible. Dogs can jump with surprising ease, so it is vital that all your fences are not just secure, but also high enough to keep your dog confined in the garden.

The height that dogs can clear depends partly on the layout. If an individual is running down a slope and can build up some momentum, then it can clear a taller fence than if it needs to head uphill. It is also possible for dogs to scramble over fences or similar solid barriers using their powerful hind legs to force them over the barrier if they get a grip on the top of it.

It may therefore be a matter of adding trelliswork on top of a brick wall for example, to raise its height. If you currently have a low mesh barrier serving as perimeter fencing in areas of your garden, then you will probably need to replace this with taller wooden fencing in anticipation of your dog's arrival.

Bear in mind that dogs can escape not just by jumping over a fence, but also by burrowing underneath it. This is a favoured route for small dogs, and particularly members of the terrier group, which will instinctively dig if they wish to get out of an area where they are confined. Block off any obvious gaps to start with, and always avoid leaving your dog out unsupervised in the garden for long periods of time.

▼ *Short-legged dogs are not necessarily easier to contain within a garden however, as terriers in particular may tunnel out.*

Car safety

Another area of your life where adjustments will need to be made for your dog is in terms of travelling in a car with your pet. If you had a dog recently, the likelihood is that you will be set up in this area, but if not, then you will need to decide on the best way forward and invest in the necessary equipment to keep both you and your dog safe.

Given the amount of traffic on roads today, it is no longer safe simply to allow your dog to sit on one of the seats while you are driving. Being momentarily distracted by your pet if it moves could easily lead to a fatal crash, and because of the danger, it is now compulsory in many countries to ensure that your dog is safely restrained when travelling in a vehicle.

The design of your car

There are various ways to keep your dog safe, influenced in part by the design of your vehicle and the size of your pet. If you have a car which

▼ *After an initial period of excitement, dogs will usually settle down on a journey, especially if they have comfortable bedding.*

opens at the rear, you may be able to have a dog guard fitted here. This is an open barrier that extends just behind the rear seat, blocking off the interior of the car, so that your dog will be securely confined in this area of the vehicle. Most car manufacturers have their own specific designs that can be retro-fitted, and some are easily removable, so that you can take them out when travelling on your own without your pet.

A guard of this type is the best option if you are acquiring a medium or large-size dog, as it will keep your pet securely confined, but you need to be aware that it may be problematic if your dog is not well-trained, unused to travelling or nervous about being in a car. The main issue that you face under these circumstances

▲ *Different designs of crates are available for travelling with your dogs. It is often better to transport two dogs individually.*

will be persuading the dog to get into the car and stay there. It is vital that you shut the back very carefully. Without much space here, there is always the associated risk of catching your dog's tail as you do so, which is likely to cause serious injury. Bear in mind, with an untrained individual, once you open the back of the car, that it could easily slip out past you and run off. This can be very dangerous for your pet, particularly if it is not yet responding well to your instructions, especially if you are parked near or on a busy road.

In the case of large dogs that are problematic to lift, and have joint ailments, then it is possible to get specially designed ramps that allow you to lead your dog up into the car directly.

It is probably not a good idea to leave your dog's leash attached while you are travelling, in case the dog becomes caught up by it, although in

◄ If you do not have a suitable vehicle to carry your dog in the rear, there are seat belts that allow you to secure your dog safely on the back seat

► In the case of older or handicapped dogs that may have difficulty in jumping up or down from a car, then you can acquire special ramps to make it easier for your pet to move back and forth.

the case of a dog that is not used to you, and displays a tendency to run off, having the leash to take hold of when cautiously opening the rear door is probably a good idea, rather than having to grab hold of its collar.

It will also be advisable to invest in a boot liner for your vehicle. These tough, rubberized trays can be lifted in and out, being ideal for dogs, especially those that may be unused to travelling in a vehicle and might be sick or soil their surroundings as a result. They also give good protection for the times when your dog becomes wet and muddy while out walking, helping to prevent the characteristic doggy odour that can otherwise accumulate in vehicles.

Carrying crates and harnesses

In the case of small dogs, a floor mat of this type can be suitable but in this instance, you may prefer to consider a carrying crate for transporting your pet, which takes up less space. These come in various designs, some of which are flat-packed, making them convenient if you tend to exercise your dog locally, and so do not drive regularly out for a walk in the countryside. These crates can double up in some cases

as carrying containers as well, being useful when you need to take your dog to the vet. It is not a good idea to keep a lead on a dog while in a container of this type, as it may wrap around its body in what is a relatively confined space. It will be easier to put your dog on its leash if it is in a carrier, because you can simply reach in and take hold of its collar without difficulty in these more confined surroundings, rather than if your pet is simply bouncing around free in the back of your car.

If you have a saloon car, then you will need to rely on using a harness for your pet instead. This fits around its body, and clips into a seatbelt socket. It is obviously very important to choose the right size of belt for your pet. Although they work well, they are not ideal for nervous dogs unused to travelling in cars. Although there is some play in the design of these seatbelts, they are essentially a restraint, and this can be an issue. Although dogs do become used to wearing them without a problem, individuals that are not familiar with travelling in a vehicle may become distressed at first. They might even soil their surroundings

as a consequence. Always make sure the car seat is protected with a durable, washable rear seat cover, in case this happens, and give your pet an opportunity to relieve itself before setting off on a journey.

Depending on the design of the seatbelt, there is a possibility that your dog might start to gnaw through the webbing, to get free. Clearly, on a short trip, this is unlikely to be successful, but you need to be aware of the risk, especially if you are aiming to drive any distance. It can also be very distracting, should your dog be howling and wriggling to free itself while you are trying to concentrate on driving.

▼ Carriers of a suitable size are ideal for smaller dogs, allowing them to be moved safely and securely.

Veterinary considerations

You will need to register with a veterinary practice, and it is worth enquiring amongst pet-owing friends which practice they use. Since all vets are expertly trained, you do not need to worry about where you go, although it may be useful to use a practice near to your home – so that you can get there quickly in an emergency, and it also makes it easier to pick up any medication.

Vets are an essential part of owning a dog as apart from specific illnesses, ongoing care will need to be given throughout your dog's life.

Neutering and vaccinations

In most cases, apart from young puppies perhaps, your dog will already have been neutered before it comes to live with you. A dog that has come from a rescue kennel will already have been vaccinated, to protect it as well as other members of the kennels from infections. You will receive details about this, in the form of a vaccination card, when your pet is handed over to you. It is likely that you will not then need to have your pet vaccinated against common infectious diseases for

▼ *Vaccinations have revolutionized dog care, making the major killer diseases a thing of the past.*

about a year but check this with the rescue centre or your own vet in due course.

The four key vaccinations usually recommended are against distemper, adenovirus (which protects against infectious canine hepatitis), canine parvovirus and leptospirosis. There are others that may be required, such as protection against rabies, depending on where you are living or if you are intending to travel overseas with your dog. Should your pet be going into kennels, then vaccination against kennel cough is recommended. Unusually, instead of being given by injection, this may be squirted up your dog's nostrils.

Fleas

Hopefully, your new pet will not bring fleas into your home, but there is always a slight risk that some of these parasites may have eluded the

centre's attempts to control them, particularly with the inevitable movements of dogs from a variety of backgrounds. Typical signs of fleas include repeated scratching and nibbling by the dog, as it tries to relieve the resulting irritation of being bitten by these parasites.

You are actually quite unlikely to spot a flea on a dog, as they move very fast through the coat, but you see signs of flea dirt, which is dark in colour and therefore easiest to identify in areas of white fur. If you are uncertain, put some of the dirt on to a white piece of paper, and splash some drops of water on it. If it dissolves, leaving a red stain, this is confirmation that your dog has indeed got fleas.

▼ *Fleas unfortunately are more prevalent than ever in centrally heated homes. Scratching is an initial common sign.*

▲ *A spot-on flea treatment. Always read and follow the instructions, double-checking that the dose is appropriate.*

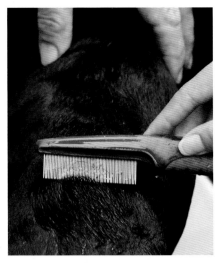

▲ *A flea comb in action, with its fine teeth dislodging the parasites from the fur and revealing flea dirt.*

There are different methods of controlling fleas, but an important piece of equipment will be a special narrow-toothed flea comb. Fleas will not be able to slip between the teeth, and so become trapped against the comb. They are still incredibly agile though, and can leap off into the home, jumping back on to your pet later. If you suspect that your dog has fleas therefore, you should always groom it outside where they will represent far less of a hazard. Keep a bucket of water nearby, and any fleas that you do encounter can be tipped in here where they cannot escape.

Fleas can multiply very rapidly in the home, typically in the vicinity of where your dog sleeps – and this may include chairs and sofas. Wash the bedding thoroughly therefore, and vacuum around the rooms where your dog goes, paying particular attention to the area in the vicinity of the skirting boards, as this is where young, developing fleas often congregate.

There are various treatments with different modes of action that you can acquire to control fleas, and often the most effective are only available on veterinary prescription. Beware if you are using flea sprays, as some of these can be harmful if not fatal to other pets, including cats and fish. So-called 'spot' treatments applied to the back of a dog's neck can help to eliminate infections by blocking the development of the flea's lifecycle, but these are not instant, knockdown solutions which will kill the fleas directly, and can be effective against ticks, which may be picked up on country walks.

Parasitic worms

A wide range of parasitic worms can infect dogs, but the common ones in the gut are divided into roundworms or tapeworms. Roundworms look rather like small white earthworms and have what is known as a direct lifecycle. This means that their eggs, which are passed out of the body in the faeces, can be spread from one dog to another, if the eggs end up contaminating a food bowl.

Tapeworms have a segmented

▶ *Some parasitic worms like* Toxocara *and* Echinococcus *are a potential threat to human health, emphasizing the need for deworming.*

appearance, with individual sections of these ribbon-like worms being voided from the dog's body, appearing like small grains of rice. They have an indirect lifecycle, having to pass through an intermediate host such as an invertebrate, which the dog must then eat for the parasite to complete its lifecycle.

Lungworms can also be a threat, and regular de-worming is the way to control these parasites, with tablets available from your vet. Similarly, in warmer parts of the world, including areas of Australia and the USA, heartworms can be an issue.

Essential equipment

Once you have a date for your rescue dog to come home, you will need to make sure you have all the equipment you will need to start off. The key essentials are food and water bowls, a collar and leash, some comfortable bedding and, if your dog is likely to feel the cold, a warm coat will be necessary for the winter months. A grooming brush will also be useful, especially for long-coated dogs.

Do not feel obligated to rush off and buy a wide range of items at the outset, as this could simply be a waste of money in some instances. Choose what your dog requires.

Food and water bowls

There is a huge range available, in a host of different designs, and your choice needs to reflect in part the size and age of your new pet. You can choose from either ceramic or heavy-duty plastic bowls, and generally, the former option is preferable on grounds of hygiene, providing the bowl does not become chipped. The interior of plastic bowls may become scratched over time, either by the dog's claws or essential regular cleaning for example, making them harder to clean subsequently.

Stability is an issue in some cases, as you do not want the bowl being

▼ *A selection of food and water bowls. Stainless steel containers can be tipped over, and the plastic ones may be chewed.*

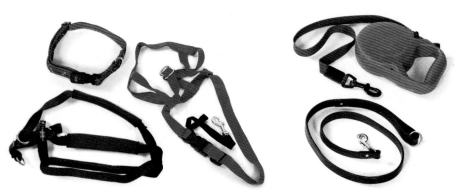

▲ *A selection of nylon collars and harnesses. It is important to choose the right size. Harnesses give more control, and protect the neck from injury, in the case of dogs that pull.*

tipped over by your dog, so check the design. Ceramic bowls with enlarged bases are harder to tip over, with this issue being increasingly important with bigger dogs. The width and depth of the bowl may be significant in spaniel-type dogs too, because of their long, heavy ears. These may dangle forwards into the bowl, and become soiled as a result. A mat for the food and water bowls can be a good investment.

An older, larger dog may find it painful to lower and extend its neck forwards to a bowl on the ground, and in these cases, you will need to invest in a raised unit. This comes in the form of a stand, with hoops in which food and water bowls are placed. Using a stand also helps to prevent the serious and potentially fatal condition known as bloat, to which big dogs are susceptible (see also page 77).

▲ *An extendable leash (top) and a leather leash (bottom). Choose a leash that feels comfortable in your hand.*

Collars and leashes

A collar and leash are also essential pieces of equipment but remember if you are starting out with a puppy, you will need to change the collar as your pet grows bigger. At the outset, it needs to fit comfortably,

▼ *A traditional broad leather hound collar. Its width helps to prevent fur underneath becoming worn.*

▲ *A variety of coats and jumpers. Some are to keep the rain off when outdoors, while others provide warmth to thin-coated and/or elderly dogs.*

▲ *The style of bed that will be most suitable for your pet depends on various factors, including its size and age.*

without being too loose so that it slides off over the puppy's head. Greyhounds, whippets and similar dogs with soft fur and a very thin undercoat require a hound collar, with the broad area helping to prevent their fur rubbing off over the neck.

These collars are made of leather, which is softer than nylon but also more expensive. Leather leashes may feel softer on the hands too, but nylon can be more durable, and is less likely to be damaged by a dog's tooth marks. It will also be unaffected by getting wet, and needs no maintenance, whereas leather does benefit from cleaning and care.

Leashes are available in different lengths. Typically, you need a medium length leash, enabling you to control your dog rather than allowing it to pull ahead. In the case of dogs that cannot be let off the leash, because their recall cannot be

trusted, then an extendable leash can be helpful. These are most useful in open countryside however, where the dog can run some distance without any risk of its leash becoming caught up around bushes.

Sleeping arrangements

A wide range of bed designs are now available, but it is not necessary to choose a bed for a puppy until it has finished teething. You are otherwise likely to find that it ends up being targeted by the young dog's teeth. Although dogs often like to curl up to sleep at times, there will also be occasions when your pet wants to stretch out instead, and so a flatter bed rather than a rigid plastic design is often a good choice, especially for larger dogs, or for older individuals and those with painful joints.

Other outdoor equipment

A towel for drying your dog off and wiping mud off its paws before it is allowed back in the car is essential. Greyhounds and similar breeds with thin coats, as well as older dogs, will

also require additional protection when the weather is inclement. There are a variety of coats available for this purpose.

In terms of the length of a dog coat, this is typically measured from the base of the neck to the base of the tail. A measurement around the base of the neck and a chest one taken just behind the forelegs are the other two measurements that are likely to be required, but ideally, take your dog along to find a coat that fits well.

There are coats that are designed to provide extra warmth, as well as other all-weather ones that will keep your dog dry. The coat may be held in place with Velcro® although nervous dogs can be disturbed by the sound of it being pulled apart, so a button fastening may be better for them. It is important that the coat does not slip, because if this happens while the dog is running, it could stumble and sustain a nasty injury.

CHAPTER THREE

BRINGING YOUR RESCUE DOG HOME

Having got your home basics ready, it will be time to collect your new companion. It is natural to feel just slightly hesitant amidst the overwhelming feeling of excitement when you bring your rescue dog home. The length of time between meeting for the first time and being able to bring your dog home does vary, depending on the individual situation and the protocols of the rescue organization concerned, but it tends to be between one to two weeks, on average. There is thus enough time to get things organized properly, in terms of what you need to do, without having to rush.

Although it may well be a new experience, especially if you haven't kept a dog before, try to avoid becoming too wrapped up in worrying about how things are going. All cases are different, and there can only be guidelines established. Be prepared for the fact that not everything will necessarily go well, but be patient, and if you encounter difficulties, don't hesitate to refer to the rescue centre for advice. Also, don't forget that it is very important at times just to stand back, and simply enjoy building up a bond with your new companion.

Time, of course, has a habit of slipping by quickly, and what you may want to do is to keep an informal journal about your dog's progress. You can subsequently look back on this and see how far you have come on your path together. It will also be nice to take some photos, and maybe share these on social media, tagging the rescue centre and thanking them for their help.

◄ *Always allow a new canine companion to have an opportunity to exercise and explore first, and then, hopefully, it will settle down on its bed.*

Paperwork practicalities

Before collecting your rescue dog there are a few formalities to consider. There will be some paperwork to complete, in terms of an agreement with the centre concerning the transfer of the dog to your care. You may be charged an adoption fee or wish to give a donation to the rescue centre to help with their ongoing work, and it is sensible to think about taking out insurance for your pet.

When you arrive to collect your dog, centre staff will be there to advise and offer support through the critical early days and weeks ahead, during the settling-in period and beyond. This support can be particularly valuable if you have not had previous experience of keeping a dog of your own before.

At the centre you will be asked to complete a handover form. This is usually a standard agreement although its contents will depend on the individual homing centre. It normally says something along the lines that the rescue centre is handing over the care of the dog to you but that the centre retains official ownership. This ensures that you have to contact them if there is a change in your circumstances and you are no longer able to look after your dog.

▲ Make sure that you have everything you need for your new companion, in advance of going to collect your pet.

▼ Leaving the centre will be a disorientating experience for your dog.

Financial matters

Rescue centres do not receive public funding, and have high running costs, in terms of looking after the dogs in their care, which often include some long-term residents that cannot be re-homed for various reasons. Fund-raising can help to defray some of these costs, but most centres now also charge adoption fees for dogs that they re-home, as a way of helping to offset all the expenses incurred in their work.

This is not a money-making exercise though; it is important to realise that these fees are unlikely even to cover all the costs of looking after your new companion while it was resident. In most cases, dogs are also neutered before leaving the centre if this has not been carried out before, and the cost of this surgery alone is likely to exceed the re-

▶ *It is a good idea to obtain pet insurance before bringing your dog home, ensuring that cover is in place from the outset.*

homing fee, as well as microchipping and other costs. Microchipping is routine and in some parts of the world, including the UK, all dogs must now be microchipped by law (see also pages 36–37).

If you are therefore able to offer a larger donation, this will be very gratefully received, and will undoubtedly help the centre to continue its work. You might also decide that you want to get involved on the fund-raising side as well.

Insurance

Depending on where you live in the world, you may be held liable for your dog's behaviour. This means that if your pet bites somebody or runs out in the road causing an accident for example, you could be made to pay compensation, which might be a very significant sum if a person has been badly injured. As a result, it is highly recommended that you take out third-party liability insurance cover.

Policies of this type may be available as an add-on at modest cost alongside your existing household insurance policy. They can even cover you if you go to a friend's house, and your dog knocks over and smashes a valuable ornament. Take care to read the small print and be certain that the cover provided meets your requirements, and that you are eligible for it. It is worth noting this is not the same type of cover that protects you if your dog

damages your home. That is simply household insurance.

Third party cover also often features in dog health insurance policies, which primarily provide a means of guarding against

▼ *Make any changes to your home, such as buying chair coverings, in advance of collecting your pet, so everything is ready.*

unexpected vet's bills. With a wide range of such policies now available, research the best one for you and your dog.

NAMING YOUR DOG

If your chosen dog has not yet got used to its name – it could be a puppy, or a stray that was named in the rescue centre – it is possible to change its name to something you would prefer.

It is important to decide on a name, not just for the purpose of bonding and future training, but also for the requisite paperwork, such as insurance, and for the engraved medallion that will be required to attach to its collar, giving a phone number as well, in case your pet strays.

This will enable you to be contacted straight away, rather than having to wait for the dog's microchip to be read.

The first few days

It really is important to try and ensure that your dog's introduction to your home goes as smoothly as possible. You are aiming to put your new pet at ease so that it can settle quickly in its new surroundings. At the beginning it is important to establish a basic routine. Mealtimes and exercise are a highly significant part of this.

Hopefully, the journey back will go well, but if your new companion is sick on the way, try not to worry. This phase will soon pass as your dog gets used to travelling by car. When you let your dog out of the vehicle, don't scold it if it has been sick. Simply put on the leash, open the back, and stroke the dog's head for reassurance, encouraging it to jump down on to the side with the pavement, so it cannot pull off into the road. If you are using a seatbelt for your pet, then once again, take the dog out on to the pavement rather than the roadside and always get into the habit of doing this for safety's sake. Should you have a small dog in a carrier, you can simply take this straight into your home.

▼ *There may be times when your dog looks a bit lost, especially in the early days. It must have space on its own.*

The initial encounter

If you can park off the road, then close any gates behind you, before opening the car to let your dog out. This in turn ensures that it should not be able to run out into the road, especially bearing in mind that it may have been poorly trained and may not respond to you at this stage.

Before going into your home, take your dog around the garden first, in the hope that it will relieve itself here. This should hopefully prevent any immediate accidents indoors. Do not rush your pet but allow it to stop and sniff as it wants. Unless it is particularly desperate, the chances are that the dog will not relieve itself immediately but will want to investigate these surroundings for a few minutes beforehand.

Talk repeatedly, using your dog's name, which should help his or her confidence, and make a fuss of your pet too, stroking it on the head after

▲ *Teach any children how to approach the dog from the start, allowing them to establish a bond together.*

it has acted as required. It will then simply be a matter of going indoors and letting your dog off the leash. After an initial period of exploration, it is quite likely that your dog may settle down and go to sleep for a period, especially after it has eaten.

Should you have children, they will, of course, be very excited about meeting the new addition to the household. Under these circumstances, assuming the weather is fine, then it will probably be best to let them meet in the garden, where the dog will not feel so confined. Encourage the children to stroke the dog individually, and not to approach from behind, which may catch it unawares and frighten it.

If they have not had a dog before, then it is very important to teach

them what to do, and to encourage them to see the world through the dog's eyes, pointing out that life can be scary for a puppy that has left its family for the first time, or indeed an older dog moving into a home where it knows no-one.

Establishing routines

It will be comforting for your dog if at least some things remain the same as they were when they were living in the rescue centre. Giving your dog the same food and at the same times will help him or her adjust to their new life with you. Once your pet is more settled, you can then alter things gradually going forwards.

▼ *With a puppy, putting a cloth which has its mother's scent on it into the sleeping area should help it settle down.*

◄ *There is a lot for a dog to learn in a new home, even simply how to ask to come in and out. Help your pet to develop a routine. It will be much harder working with a street dog that has never been used to such restrictions on its movement before.*

Try to establish a night-time routine as well, and initially at least, go out with your dog even if you do not head out for a walk as such. This gives an opportunity to build the bond further, as you can call the dog to you, and so you can start to train it to come back indoors. Furthermore, you can check that it has relieved itself, so that it should then settle down for the night, without any accidents.

Probably the best place to encourage your dog to sleep at night will be in the kitchen, as it will be warm, there will be nothing that can be damaged very easily, and if an accident happens overnight, it will be much easier to clear up here than in other parts of the house.

It is a good idea, at least initially, to take your dog out for a walk so that it will be reasonably tired when you are wanting to go to bed and should then settle down without a problem. You may find, however, that your dog does wake up and make some noise during the night. This is one time when you really need to harden your heart, resisting the urge to go and allow your pet to come and sleep in your bedroom.

Dogs can be arch manipulators in this situation, and what began as being an arrangement for one or two nights can rapidly extend to years, becoming an unforeseen permanent arrangement!

ACCESS TO CHAIRS

Another decision that will need to be taken at the outset is whether or not you want your dog to be allowed up onto comfy chairs and sofas.

Drawbacks to allowing your dog on to chairs include stains from muddy paws, unpleasant doggy odour and loose dog's hair on your furniture. What you can do is to cover them with suitable throws, which will keep your pet away from the actual material of the chair. These can be washed easily, to prevent the build-up of any doggy odour, and removed when you have visitors.

Taking the time to regularly groom your dog to remove loose hair will make it easier to keep the house tidy. If you have a leather sofa or a similar covering that could be damaged by your dog's claws, then it will be essential to protect the surface. This is primarily because of the way that dogs settle down to sleep, by scratching first at the surface beneath them, and then going round in a circle before lowering themselves down on to the spot.

If you decide that you do not want your dog to sit on a chair or sofa, then provide a comfortable bed for your pet nearby, and be consistent from the outset. Do not initially allow your dog up onto your chairs and then decide a month later, once your pet is settled, that it is no longer acceptable. Consistency in training is key.

The importance of house-training

Certain categories of rescue dog, such as ex-racing greyhounds and individuals rescued from puppy farms, that will have spent all their lives in kennels are unlikely to be instinctively clean in the home. Puppies too are likely to fall into this category, so you will need to be prepared for some accidents around the home, particularly during the early days.

◄ Encourage your dog to go into the garden regularly through the day, as a way of stopping it from soiling in the home.

After it has finished, always praise your pet when it performs as required outdoors, giving it the opportunity to go back indoors again straightaway if it wishes. Your dog may prefer to explore for a few minutes in the garden first, however, before returning.

Be certain to clean up thoroughly after your dog, particularly if children will have access to the garden. Regular deworming is also vital, to minimize any risk of toxocariasis, as the *Toxocara* worm eggs can be transmitted to people, with potentially serious consequences.

When it comes to house-training your dog, you need to develop a routine to ensure that there will be no reason for your pet to soil in the home. Start by letting your dog out into the garden or taking it for a walk first thing in the morning. Then subsequently, about every two hours or so through the day, allow your dog to relieve itself again in the garden. It often helps if you go out with the dog in the early stages, so that you can be sure that is acting as required.

Otherwise, particularly if it is cold or wet, greyhounds will simply run around very briefly and then ask to come back inside again, having done nothing. This then greatly increases the likelihood that they will soil somewhere in the home as a result.

It is a particularly good idea to give your dog an opportunity to relieve itself outside soon after it has eaten, as this will trigger the movement of the gut and is likely to result in defecation.

▼ If a puppy soils or wets in the home, it is often your fault! Put your puppy outside about every two hours during the day.

When absent from home
Most dogs will rapidly adapt to a routine, finally being taken out last thing at night just before you go to

▼ Clear up thoroughly after your dog, and make sure it is regularly dewormed, so it cannot spread toxocariasis.

▲ *Always head out with poo bags so you can clear up after your pet if it relieves itself when you are out for a walk.*

bed. A difficulty may arise, however, when you are out for much of the day. It is unreasonable to expect your dog to be clean over this length of time, and ideally, you may be able to arrange for someone to let your dog out at lunchtime as a minimum.

Alternatively, another option that may be worth investigating, before you require their services, are doggy daycare services in your area. These may operate in slightly different ways, but typically, you can drop your dog off here in the morning, and the staff will look after your pet during the day while you are away from home.

The service may not be suitable for all dogs, particularly nervous individuals, or those with disabilities, but equally, it can be invaluable if you find yourself stuck without any help for a day. It also provides an opportunity for your dog to socialize and play with others in a supervised environment.

Most puppies are unlikely to learn to ask to go out when they want to relieve themselves until they are at least six months of age. With older dogs that have previously spent their time in kennels, the time interval to reach this stage will vary, but almost certainly, it will probably still be a few months rather than just a couple of weeks.

Indoor accidents

The aim should always be to prevent accidents, and there is no point scolding your dog when it does soil indoors. This will be counterproductive, on the basis that dog will not understand what it has done wrong, and this can seriously weaken the bond of trust that you are trying to build up between you.

When an accident does happen, the key is to prevent any recurrence. You need to clear up thoroughly, obviously on grounds of hygiene, but equally, to deter your dog returning to this spot in the future, which could otherwise be an issue. Certain disinfectants, such as those with a pine scent, may reinforce rather than eliminate the scent to the dog's nose. It is much better to acquire a special product that both disinfects and eliminates the scent.

OUTDOOR PROBLEMS

If you are finding that you are having problems in the garden, with the dog relieving itself in areas that you would rather were not used for this purpose, there are other products that should hopefully attract your dog to the area where they are used. A common issue is linked with bitches, because their urine is more acidic than male dogs and can kill off areas of grass in a lawn as a result. Treatments to attract the dog off the grass, on to a nearby paved area perhaps, can be obtained online or in pet stores. Beware though, because their effectiveness may be short-lived when it rains, and a further treatment will need to be applied.

▼ *You may need to persuade your dog to use another part of your garden if you find that your lawn is being killed off.*

Another pet in the house

Just as a new dog will need to get used to you, so it will also need to adjust to other pets that you may have, such as another dog or a cat, and you will need to take particular care with those which could be viewed as prey species, typically small pets, such as rabbits or guinea pigs. Ensure their quarters are adequately secured and located out of reach as far as possible.

Careful preparation is the key if you already have a pet and are seeking to integrate another dog to live in harmony alongside it.

Issues around two dogs

Some dogs, notably those with a scent hound ancestry, such as basset hounds, are naturally more social than others, like terriers, which are much more territorial, despite their relatively small size. Age can also play a part, with an older dog often being more inclined to accept a puppy, and if either individual was living with another dog previously, introductions should be easier.

Should you already have a resident dog, start by taking the two dogs out for a walk together – but don't confine them in the car at this stage,

especially if they have not met before. Hopefully, after a good walk without being let off to run, they will both be tired and inclined to sleep when they get home. Although counter-intuitive, harmony is most likely to be achieved by reinforcing the position of the established dog in

▲ *Mealtimes are likely flashpoints, particularly if one dog eats its food more quickly than its companion.*

the canine hierarchy over the days ahead, rather than trying to reassure the newcomer.

The key flashpoints are likely to be around food, and secondly concerning toys, so you will need to plan accordingly. Never feed the dogs in the same room, as one will probably finish eating its own food earlier than the other, at which point it may well seek to steal some of its companion's, which is likely to elicit an aggressive reaction. There will be little time to step in under these circumstances, as the other dog will react quickly, by snarling and striking out, seeking to drive its companion away.

In the case of toys, the reaction is usually less intense, but it rather

▼ *When dogs are playing together, you need to be careful, as some dogs can be very possessive about toys.*

▶ *A dog will obviously need to become acquainted with a cat sharing the same home but beware that all may not go well at first.*

depends on the circumstances. If one dog picks up the other dog's toy while it is resting perhaps, then the chances of an aggressive reaction are reduced, compared with a situation where the newcomer tries to take the toy from its companion, which will be perceived as a direct challenge.

There are several things that you can do to prevent conflict under these circumstances. Firstly, be sure that the dogs have a good choice of toys, keeping these in a toy basket that is readily accessible, so they can wander over and pick one out when they feel like it. Bear in mind that each is likely to have one or two favourites though you will probably not be able to predict which!

Secondly, play with the dogs separately at first, so that the risk of any competition spilling over into conflict will be eliminated. In addition, if the dogs are markedly different in size or appearance, then the likelihood of them wanting to play in the same way will be reduced. Nevertheless, the possibility of disputes over chew-type toys will remain. Over time, you may find that they start playing together.

Issues around cats

This can be a much trickier encounter, given the fact that most cats will not be overjoyed to have a dog intruding into their serene existence. Avoid forcing them together but let them meet on their own terms. Cats can strike up quite a close friendship with

some dogs over time, but there can be no guarantees in this respect. It is very much a personal thing between the two of them and could go either way. What you do not want is for your new dog to chase your cat on a regular basis, as this will get things off on a very negative footing, although a cat will often bring a puppy into line on its own accord by suddenly stopping, turning round, and hissing menacingly at its pursuer.

In due course, a cat may come to appreciate the advantages of having a canine companion in its life, if it deters the neighbourhood cats from invading its space, and brings help if it finds itself cornered, as dogs can recognize the calls made by cats that share the home with them. Equally, dogs may deter larger, potentially aggressive predators such as foxes from setting up home in the garden.

Dangers to other pets

It is very important to keep other pets well away from your dog, either indoors or outside. Rabbits are the natural quarry of several hound breeds, and, if nothing else, they will be very frightened by a dog just outside their hutch or run. Guinea pigs and similar creatures are also vulnerable, and there can be other less obvious targets, in the guise of tortoises or chickens for example, both of which can be badly injured

and even killed by a dog in a matter of seconds, so take no chances.

Neighbourhood dogs

If you live in an urban area, the likelihood is that your dog will not be the only one around. As a result, you are likely to find that your dog may be drawn into a chorus of barking. The situation can be even worse if there is another dog next door, as the likelihood is that it will start to scrap across the fence, and if it is an open mesh fence, allowing the dogs to see each other, then the situation will be worse.

It may be better to speak with your neighbour, and think about putting up a wooden panel fence, so hopefully the dogs will be inclined to lose interest in each other. There should also be no risk of one dog biting the other badly on the face, and especially around the nose, or scratching their eyes.

▼ *Just because your dog looks cute does not mean that it may not harm other pets like this tortoise.*

Meeting visitors

Behaving well when meeting new people is something that is very important, in terms of socializing your dog. During the early few days, however, you should allow your dog to settle down and find its way around the home with few, if any interruptions, especially if it is not used to being social, or is known to be nervous by nature because of bad experiences with people in the past.

Dogs generally will bark when someone knocks at the door, as a way of alerting you to the person's presence. What you do not want is for the dog to continue barking, or to react aggressively when a friend comes into your home. Some breeds tend to be more territorial than others, having been bred as guardians. People tend to focus on members of this group, such as Rottweilers, which are also quite large dogs. Yet it is often overlooked that several small breeds such as Pekingese also served in part as guardians, and although they are very friendly and loyal to people in their immediate circle, they are

◄ Dogs are always alert, whether picking up on the sound of another dog in the neighbourhood barking or detecting a strange voice in your home, thanks to their keen hearing.

naturally suspicious of strangers, and can display a tendency to continue barking when they are in the home, to everyone's annoyance.

What you need to achieve is a balance whereby your dog alerts you to the arrival of someone at the door, and then settles down again, whether the person is invited into your home or not. It will take time to reach this situation, and you will need to take the initiative, in persuading your dog that nothing is wrong.

Meeting people indoors

When someone comes into your home, and you go to sit down, make sure that your pet comes and sits with you at this stage, so you can give it some reassuring pats, encouraging it to calm down and settle (see also pages 132 and 165).

It is likely that your dog will want to introduce itself, and this will then make it more likely to ignore your visitors subsequently. Assuming they are happy therefore, let the dog meet them close-up, and perhaps give it a few friendly pats initially by way of an introduction.

▼ Most dogs like to see what is going on – particularly if there is any hint of food – but often lose interest.

▼ Dogs can become overexcited and even aggressive when a visitor calls. It is important to prevent such behaviour.

▲ You may need to keep your dog on a leash at first, if it proves to be a constant nuisance when people come round.

You do face more of a difficulty if your dog is instinctively nervous and wary, holding back and displaying signs of uncertainty, in terms of body language. Its ears may be drawn back, and its tail is likely to be tucked down. If approached, the dog will lower its body closer to the ground and roll over.

On the other hand, if after a while, it feels there is no threat and wants to be more friendly, then it may stand with one paw slightly raised off the ground. This confirms that it is still uncertain whether to go forwards or back. Provided that your friend is welcoming though, then the chances are that your pet can be won over and will soon approach more closely.

Meeting people outdoors

It can be easier to meet outside in a garden, as the dog will feel more confident here, because there is space to run off, but even so, you do

not want your dog misbehaving and making a nuisance of itself, so after an initial run round, encourage your pet to come and sit on the ground alongside you.

The situation can be more difficult if there are children involved, as they will probably want to play with your dog especially outdoors in the garden. Yet this may be the first encounter that you have had with

▼ You need to ensure that your dog will sit with you or go off and sleep in its bed after having greeted a visitor.

▲ Dogs are very alert, and your pet will learn the sound of your doorbell, asking to come inside to meet your guest.

your dog involving children, if you have none of your own. You may also be uncertain as to how it will react under these circumstances.

The safest option therefore will be not to encourage them to play together for a long period of time, although if you know that your pet likes chasing after a ball, you could allow a child to throw this so your dog can collect it. What you do not want is for the child to try and take the ball off your pet however, if the dog is not keen to drop it.

Dropping a ball is usually something that dogs learn very quickly, if they wish to carry on playing, but with a young child, you must make certain that they do not try to grab the ball near the dog's mouth, so always supervise such games closely. Although it may not do it aggressively, simply seeing it as part of the game, your dog could try to grab the ball, and end up catching the child's hand with its teeth instead.

CHAPTER FOUR

A DEVELOPING RELATIONSHIP

One of the great joys of having a dog is that by nature, dogs are uplifting to be around. Even if they have had a terrible start in life, as can apply to many rescue dogs, they generally retain a positive spirit, and can be won round and blossom when shown care and commitment. Obviously, this cannot be achieved instantly, but generally, the more time that you can invest in getting to understand your new companion, and work to build up a bond between you, the quicker that you will see progress.

As with all pets, general care in terms of feeding and grooming will be important. Yet there can be longer term issues that will need addressing, if your dog is in any way disabled because of its previous life or is suffering from a chronic ailment. There are more options than ever, in terms of complementary health care to assist under these circumstances, not to mention technological advances as well, to help your dog live as full and as active a life as possible.

The first step that marks very clear progress in bonding with your pet will be when your dog's training has advanced to the extent that you can look forward to allowing it off the leash for periods when you are out walking together. It may be that your dog is still rather shy though, so try to persuade friends and relatives calling round to make a point of saying hello to your pet. Hopefully, as it meets more people, so your pet will gain in confidence, rather than hiding away, and will soon be happy to settle down from the outset and sit close to visitors.

◄ *Choosing where and when to allow your dog off the leash is an important decision and marks a significant advance in your relationship.*

Beginning training

You will gain an insight into your dog's behaviour very quickly, and will soon see how much training is required for your dog to become truly responsive. Dogs are, by nature, keen to please and they are always learning. Treat every interaction as an opportunity to train your dog. What you are aiming for is to train your dog to do what you want it to do, while counteracting or deterring it from developing bad habits.

Before beginning any training it will be worthwhile discussing your dog's training requirements with the rescue centre, and ideally with an accredited behaviourist, as they will probably be able to guide you to a local instructor who may be most suitable to assist. You must do the hard work yourself, however, under their guidance, simply because your dog needs to respond to you, rather than a third party who will not be present outside training sessions. Even if you have very little or no prior experience training a dog beforehand, be reassured that help will be at hand if

▼ *Play provides not just a good way to bond with your pet, but also to teach basic commands such as 'fetch' or 'drop'.*

▲ *Ideally, dogs really need to be taught on their own at first, to ensure that they are focusing on what is required.*

you need it, with various dog-training groups operating in many towns.

Training guidelines

When doing any training, it is important to appreciate that just as dogs rely heavily on their body language to reflect their mood, so you too need to be prepared to use both verbal and non-verbal means of communication. Some breeds (and resulting crosses) are easier to train than others, and there is no doubt that it is easier to start training a puppy than an older dog that may be set in its ways or has had very little training previously.

Key guidelines for successful training include being able to communicate clearly and effectively with your dog. If it becomes confused, it will lose focus and will then be unsure what is required. A key aspect of clear communication is encouraging your dog to recognize the sound of your voice and its name. Always talk to your dog by using its name, so that it comes to identify with it. A dog that has lived in a home before will have become familiar with its name, but in the case of a young puppy, or an older stray, then they may not yet have identified with their name.

Patience is also necessary – just like us, dogs can have off-days: on one day, things may go really well, while subsequently, your dog may seem to have slipped back a bit. Always

remember that training is not a linear progression – there will be bumps along the road, but overall, your dog should be making progress over time.

Mastering the basics

There are certain vital lessons that all dogs must learn, starting with 'sit'. You do not want your dog jumping up at every opportunity and bounding around, if for no other reason than it makes it hard to put its leash on when necessary. You also want your pet to 'drop', letting go of items that it perhaps should not have picked up in the first place. When out walking, you want your dog to 'stay' when instructed, and always to 'come' when called.

You can reinforce these verbal commands with hand signals,

◄ Some dogs find it easier to adopt certain postures, such as begging, than others. In this case, the dog sits up, encouraged by the offer of a treat. This is more difficult for long-bodied dogs like greyhounds.

holding the palm of your hand upright and pointing towards your dog for example, reinforcing the 'stay' command. Then, when you want your dog to return to you, turn your hand round and motion the dog to return to you. (For more detailed advice on basic training see pages 162–171).

Training sessions should always be focused and yet fun for your dog. Its powers of concentration will be limited, however, so it is better to keep the sessions short. But each training session can be repeated several times during the day. To be effective, training needs to be carried out in an environment where there are no distractions. It will be one thing training your dog on your own in your garden, but quite another if your children are kicking a football around here as well.

A garden will make an ideal training ground at first, but in due course, you will want to repeat these sessions in an area where you take your dog regularly for a walk. Here again, a quiet time of the day for these sessions is to be recommended.

▲ You can train your dog to do tricks too, such as finding the treat in this case, by using observation and scent.

TREATS AND TRAINING

There are lots of different treats now commercially available for dogs, which can be incorporated into the training process. But they are not essential, and with the growing number of dogs that are now overweight or even obese, it is important to be aware of your dog's weight, and not add unnecessarily to its calorific intake. it may be a good idea to opt for low calorie treats, such as a small, diced piece of sweet apple or carrot, both of which dogs will generally eat quite readily. Be particularly careful over the use of treats if your dog is diabetic and speak with your vet about what would be suitable. The most immediate concern is, however, that the over-use of treats can be counterproductive. You may find that your dog simply becomes fixated on the treat, rather than on the training process itself. It can also be hard work phasing out edible rewards so use your treats wisely. (For more information on phasing out treats see page 171).

▲ Offering a treat during training will encourage your dog to concentrate.

Ongoing training

It varies as to how long it will take for your dog to respond to you, because this will depend largely upon its background. Encourage other members of your family to get involved in your pet's care, so that when you are away for example, your dog will know the routine and will not feel confused. A clicker is an useful aid, helping to prevent over-reliance on treats during training and subsequently.

◄ Part of taking your dog out at first will be learning how it reacts in different situations, including meeting other dogs.

and whether you need to repeat the instructions. This will give you some insight into the progress that your pet is hopefully making.

Using a clicker

Another important way to communicate with your dog and show how well it is doing, in terms of appreciating what is required, will be to obtain a special clicker. This is a very simple mechanical device, available from pet stores or online, that operates purely on sound. It doesn't preclude you from praising your pet, which you should always

The responsiveness of an individual dog depends on several factors, starting with the breed ancestry of your pet. Companion-type dogs are likely to respond most quickly, particularly if they are still relatively young, whereas at the other end of the spectrum, those of sighthound origins can be more problematic. It is not that they are unwilling to bond with you, as they usually have enthusiastic, friendly natures, but they also possess a strong independent streak as well. Making training fun, so the dog wants to participate, is also important.

An honest assessment

Measuring the hopeful improvement in your dog's responsiveness since you acquired it is important, so you can assess the progress that you are making together. It helps if each week, you can have a set series of

exercises that you can run through together, ideally at the same time of day, involving the key components of the initial training such as 'sit', 'stay' and 'drop', as well as testing your pet's powers of recall. You can see how spontaneously these actions are carried out, and how long they take,

▼ Aim to encourage your dog to focus on you when you are out together. Start by talking to get your pet's attention.

do when it responds as required, but instead, it serves to reinforce this message.

Before using this training tool however, you must have mastered the basics satisfactorily with your dog first. This is because you will sometimes be giving a treat as a reward, but not straight away. What you emphatically don't want is for your dog to jump up and simply aim to seize the treat out of your hand, partly because there is a real risk that you will end up being bitten as a result.

Dogs that are possessive about food, often because they were teased with titbits or even their food bowl in the past, are most likely to behave in this way, so as a precaution, it may be a good idea to resort to clicker training initially after your pet has had a meal. This is likely to take the edge off its hunger, lessening the risk that it will try to snatch the treat from you.

How the clicker works

When you are teaching your dog to sit, for example, start out with a treat which you hold close to your dog's nose, then once it has detected the food item, lift it up over your dog's head, instructing it to sit, which it will do almost instinctively as it wants to focus on the treat above it. When the dog acts as instructed, use the click straight away, to indicate that it has done what was required, and then reward it with the treat.

DID YOU KNOW?
The big advantage of clicker training is that you can use this not just to teach your pet to sit, but for other training as well, creating complex routines in this way. Indeed, those teaching what is strictly called 'heelwork to music', but what is much more widely referred to simply as 'doggy dancing', frequently use clicker training to put together routines with their pets.

▶ *Dogs can be taught using clicker training, whether as part of everyday training or for competition purposes.*

Carry on in this way, repeating the exercise and move away slightly, so the dog needs to follow you. Wait for it to sit again and click immediately. The reason for doing this simultaneously with the action is that the dog will associate them together, and appreciate that it has done the right thing, for which it may be rewarded with a treat.

The one thing that you don't want to do is to end up in a situation where you are hostage to giving treats every time. The dog's focus will otherwise tend to shift to the reward, rather than the action. As things progress therefore, always use the sound of the clicker, but only give a treat intermittently, which helps to maintain your dog's concentration.

▼ *Keeping a dog's concentration is vital during training sessions, so it can learn without being distracted.*

Regular exercise

Taking your dog out regularly every day is important, to provide it with both physical and mental exercise. But when you start, choose the location carefully. Do not go to a crowded park for example, where there will be lots of other dogs, not to mention children playing with balls. There are many potential difficulties that you will need to negotiate, even if you keep your dog on its leash.

When you start going out walking, it may be a good idea to obtain a muzzle for your dog, if it is nervous. A dog will often react aggressively if another individual which is running free comes up close while it is on a leash, as it feels trapped. Sadly, many owners do not appreciate this, and fail to keep their dogs under control, preventing them from behaving in this fashion. Ideally, plan instead to find somewhere where you are likely to have more space to yourselves.

Whenever you want to cross a road, always get your dog to sit back slightly back from the kerb, so that this becomes second nature, while you wait for passing traffic to clear, allowing you to cross safely. It can be useful to start by walking your dog on the streets around your home, so it can get used to sights and sounds here. You can also encourage your dog to walk well on its lead, keeping it walking in a straight line to your side, and not pulling ahead.

When you start exercising your dog in a more rural environment carry on running through the same training instructions that you have been using previously. This is where a leash that can be extended and retracted can be very valuable, as you can let the dog go a greater distance from you, before calling it back and shortening the leash again. You can even try dipping out of sight, and ask your dog to come and find you, encouraging it to come running back and then sit as instructed.

One of the advantages of using an extendable leash is that the dog will cover up to twice as much ground as you will, as it runs back and forth. Nevertheless, there will also be times on the walk when you want to concentrate on training your dog to walk well alongside you on a leash, and it can just be shortened for this purpose.

Provided the ground is relatively open, so an extendable leash will not

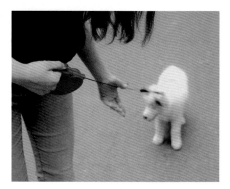

▲ *There are likely to be times, especially in busy or noisy locations, where your dog may hang back because it is nervous.*

get caught up, you can also carry on training your dog to chase after and return with a ball or similar toy, although obviously the level of activity needs to reflect the age and the physical capabilities of the dog concerned. But dogs can be remarkably adaptable, and even in cases where an individual has sadly had to have a leg amputated, once it has adapted to this change, it is still likely to enjoy chasing after a ball.

◄ *Most dogs enjoy running on an empty sandy beach but ensure your pet cannot pick up and swallow shells or pebbles.*

▼ *Extendable leashes offer a good way for your dog to exercise, especially before it can be allowed to run free.*

▲ *Young and active dogs will benefit from a safe exercise area where they can run and jump.*

▲ *Dogs should not be exercised in the midday sun. Those with short muzzles are at greatest risk of heat stroke.*

▲ *There are special drinking bottles that you can buy for your pet and take with you when you are out on a walk.*

Individual exercise requirements

The amount of exercise required depends on the type of dog, and its physical state of health as well. A dog that has been starving and weak, or has had to undergo major surgery, will obviously require less exercise than usual until it is restored to full health.

The rescue centre will be able to advise you on the length of walk required. Certainly, if your dog feels that it has gone far enough, it will start to hang back and may even sit down. When playing, once it has had enough, a dog may simply walk away.

When out walking, and certainly if the weather is warm, offer your dog a drink of water. There are combined water-bottle drinkers that you can fit to a belt so that you can carry them hands-free, while you are out on the walk. This will help to deter your pet attempting to drink from muddy puddles that could be polluted with any chemical run-off, and from ponds which may contain harmful toxic algae.

You will very soon get an insight into how much exercise your dog needs, and usually after a walk of any length, and especially if this is followed by a meal, your dog will then go to sleep. Dogs generally need at least one good walk a day, always avoiding the heat of the

THE DANGERS OF BLOAT

Never be tempted to feed your dog before going out for a walk or before playing with your pet. Large dogs that are commonly encountered in rescues, including greyhounds or lurcher-type dogs which are characterized by their

▼ *Vigorous exercise soon after a meal predisposes dogs to the serious risk of bloat. Plan your pet's walks to avoid this danger.*

midday sun when it is shining, or even two shorter ones, which is a better option especially if a dog is building up its strength again.

deep, narrow chests, are particularly vulnerable to the condition known as bloat.

The stomach, with the weight of food in it, can easily shift position within the abdomen and become painfully twisted. Successful treatment is difficult and is likely to involve fairly major surgery. It is also better for this reason to feed these dogs several times during the day, rather than just providing one large meal.

Letting your dog off the leash

When you finally let your dog off the leash it is an exciting day, after all the preparation and training that has gone into reaching this stage. It is hard to predict the right time to allow your pet to run free for the first time. There are several criteria that need to be met, but the most important is that you feel confident that even if your dog does run off after something, it will come back to you when called.

Make sure that your dog is familiar with the paths through the area where you have been walking regularly, before letting it off the leash. Choose a fine day for this, because if your dog does disappear, it may find it easier to retrace its steps to you under these conditions, rather than in the rain. Take the clicker and some treats as you carry on the training process in these familiar surroundings. Choose a location well away from sheep and other livestock.

Stay alert!

Once you are far enough away from the road, simply detach the leash from your dog's collar. The likelihood is that it will not immediately dash off, even if it has an athletic nature. The dog may be more likely just to pause for a few moments, sniffing around while you carry on down the path. Ignore your pet if it does this at first, but if it does not follow you, pause and call it to you. Avoid walking back because you want the dog to come to you in these circumstances.

Ideally, you should be in a situation when your dog is never out of your sight, although this can become more difficult in wooded areas. Try to avoid letting it get too far in front of you. What is very important is to carry on the training, and call your dog back to you regularly, and by so doing, you retain your dog's focus, and keep control of your pet.

▲ *Building a bond with your dog is vital, in encouraging it to come back to you when you first allow it off the leash.*

You can never be entirely sure what you may encounter – deer may emerge on to the path ahead of you, or a horse and rider may unexpectedly start cantering down the track. Whatever happens, you need to be confident that you can always retain control over your dog, even when the unexpected occurs, and it returns to your side without hesitation.

Keeping practising recall with your dog at regular intervals during the walk, using the clicker and the occasional treat. The other aspect of training that is particularly important when you are out walking with your pet is to ensure that it sits when instructed, even if you are some distance away at the time.

This is crucial in a situation where it is not practical to call your dog to you, allowing you to get to its position, and to ensure that you can put your dog back on its leash easily, rather than having to catch it by the collar as it darts around excitedly in

▼ *Although you will have practiced recall with your dog at home, there will be lots of distractions once it is roaming free.*

▶ If your dog is energetic, go for a walk to tire it before letting it run free. Go through training exercises just as you would at home, using a clicker for example to persuade it to sit at times.

front of you. (For more advice on 'sit' and recall training see pages 164 and 166.)

What not to do...

Do not chase after your dog if it does run off, perhaps having spotted a rabbit, for example. Stand your ground, and simply call your dog back to you calmly, even if at first, it fails to respond. Running off after it will reinforce the sense of a chase for your pet, with hound-type dogs such as greyhounds or lurchers being most likely to respond in this way. After some distance, however, when the animal disappears into the undergrowth, your dog will simply sniff around in that area for a short time and lose interest.

There is always a risk that in more urban areas, your pet may be confronted by another dog. If your pet is known not to agree well with

▼ A high-pitched dog whistle, which your pet has become familiar with beforehand, can be very useful on walks.

other dogs, then ensure that it wears a muzzle, so that it can cause no harm under these circumstances. Conversely of course, there is a risk that it could be effectively ambushed by another individual, but with your dog walking near you, you can call it back easily if this happens.

Whistling

This is the stage in the training process when you can introduce a special high-frequency dog whistle to your dog, which will probably be inaudible to you. Having called your pet, give, say, three successive blasts on the whistle. Dogs have a hearing range which is much wider than our own and they can detect sounds that are above our hearing frequency.

A whistle of this type will allow you to keep in touch with your dog over a long distance, and if it does stray off and get lost, the sound of the whistle will help it to locate you more easily and return. By using the whistle on a regular basis, and giving the same blast, your dog will soon come to recognize the sound and should start responding to it. You can even use it in the garden to start familiarizing your dog to the sound.

BE PREPARED

When out walking through the countryside, especially during the winter months, your dog is likely to end up quite muddy on its underparts. This can be a particular issue with dogs that have relatively long hair on the backs of their legs, known as 'feathering', which can attract a decent amount of mud. It is quite easy to get this out of the coat, however, without having to wash your dog in hot soapy water. Constant bathing is not really to be recommended, as it will strip the natural oils out of the coat.

Keep a special doggy towel in the boot of the car and use this to wipe off obvious mud on your dog's legs and paws when you get back to your vehicle, or on your doorstep if you walked from home. Then simply wait for the rest to dry, which will be a quicker process than you might have imagined, at which point, you can simply brush the remaining mud out of the coat.

Reacting to the great outdoors

Walking your dog in the countryside is an enjoyable and rewarding experience but there are legal considerations that must be met, and you need to stay alert to the potential dangers that you may encounter. Some animals, such as sheep, can be seriously harassed by a dog off a lead, even causing pregnant ewes to abort. Other animals, such as cattle, pigs and snakes can be a danger to your pet.

It helps if you prepare directly by visiting a quiet area of countryside in the build-up to this period, keeping your dog on the leash, and at the same time, being sure that it should be as safe as possible, just in case your dog does not prove to be as responsive as it has been up to this stage. You need to be able to walk some distance off and away from the passing road, before you think about letting your dog off, so it needs to be quite a large area, ideally in a quiet location.

COUNTRYSIDE CODE

Local laws regarding dogs and the countryside will change depending on where you live but the following guidelines should be followed at all times.

• Always keep your dog on a lead or in sight.

• Be confident your dog will return on command.

• Make sure your dog does not stray from the path or area where you have right of access. Always check local signs as there are situations when you must keep your dog on a leash for all or part of the year. Some local areas may also ban dogs completely, except for assistance dogs.

It is good practice wherever you are to keep your dog on a lead around livestock. In the UK on Open Access land and at the coast, you must put your dog on a lead around any livestock. A farmer can shoot a dog that is attacking or chasing his or her livestock. Always check the local regulations.

Contact with livestock and wild animals

One thing that you will not have been able to work out is how your dog responds to the presence of farm stock. Dogs can be aggressive when they encounter sheep, and it is emphatically not sensible to walk in the vicinity of any fields where there could be sheep. You would normally keep your dog on the leash in such areas, as a precautionary measure. Dogs that attack sheep can be identified by their DNA if necessary and destroyed, leaving owners liable to pay compensation.

There is the risk that if you allow your pet off its leash and its runs away then it may end up straying into a field of sheep and causing havoc, so caution is definitely advisable. Any dog can turn on sheep, although ironically, it is probably collie-type dogs that are most like to behave in this way. It may well reflect their herding instincts having become seriously warped – they expect the sheep to behave in a particular way, but then they fail to do so, and the dog reacts aggressively, feeling overwhelmed by the frustration of not being able to control the flock.

Dogs are less likely to respond aggressively if they enter a field of cattle. In fact, they themselves are

▼ *Make sure that your dog is on a leash in an area where you are likely to come across domestic livestock such as sheep.*

► *Always be careful introducing your dog to a horse, and keep your pet tightly restrained on the leash. Never walk around the back of the horse as this is especially dangerous.*

▲ *A dog running free in a field of cattle can cause a stampede. It may even be attacked, especially by cows with calves.*

likely to be in greater danger in these surroundings, particularly if the herd comprises cows with calves, or young bullocks, which can be rather skittish at certain times of year. Sadly, every year, dogs are trampled to death by cattle, and it is worth emphasizing an aggressive reaction can result even if you are simply crossing a field with your dog on its leash. Be on constant alert under these circumstances as to how the cattle are reacting, and do not end up trapped in the corner of the field.

Pigs, too, can be aggressive if they feel under threat, and they possess powerful teeth, and even tusks in some cases. The biggest risk, however, are wild boar in parts of the UK and some areas of Europe, and the wild populations of pigs now breeding across much of the USA and Australia. Although shy by nature, these free-living pigs are very aggressive, and sows especially will kill dogs if they feel their piglets are in danger.

Other potential dangers

Depending on where you live, there can be other hazards too. Venomous snakes are to be found in many countries, with the threat varying from almost zero in the UK through to Australia at the other extreme, which is home to the deadliest snakes in the world. Both the USA and Australia are also home to various crocodilians, which are a danger to dogs. The answer in this case is not to let your dog get close to the water's edge, within striking distance of these reptiles.

Even in areas where crocodiles are absent, it is still not a good idea to choose a path close to a river, or

indeed the sea, because of potentially powerful currents or tides. Many dogs can swim well instinctively, but they can still drown if for any reason, such as chasing waterfowl, they plunge in the water and are swept away. It is also obviously not a good idea to let your dog roam free on cliff tops either.

Once you are confident that your dog will return to you every time when called, these issues become less significant. You can simply slip your dog back on its leash and walk away from any potential danger. That is why it is so important to reach this position with your dog, with ongoing training.

◄ *Depending on where you are, be alert to the risk of your dog encountering a venomous snake or other potentially dangerous wildlife, especially when it is off the leash, and always look out for any possible risks that may lie on the route ahead.*

How technology can help

Depending how hi-tech you want to be, there are GPS trackers available for dogs. Fitting one of these to your pet's collar will not stop it from running off, but it will indicate exactly where your pet is. So if your dog disappears when you are out on a walk, you should be able to follow its movements and catch it before any harm results. Some trackers also monitor your dog's activity levels .

Lightweight trackers are designed to attach to the collar, being relatively unobtrusive, as well as robust. They are not easily knocked off, although this is something that you should check prior to purchase, as some designs attach more effectively than others. The units are waterproof, continuing to work either in a rainstorm or if your dog plunges into water. There are different models available, and the technology in this area is continuing to be developed, so it is worthwhile looking at the

▼ *Young, exuberant dogs may run off quickly and disappear, especially in wooded areas, losing touch with you.*

range of different options and what else they offer, aside from being able to find your dog if it strays on a walk. You can find a wide selection online – these devices tend to be less commonly stocked by pet stores.

Some units allow you to cover a specific area, alerting you immediately if your dog strays from this zone, which is obviously useful as it indicates straightaway if it has escaped from the vicinity of your garden and is heading off elsewhere. The GPS tracker can also act as an activity monitor, seeing how much exercise your pet is taking, combined with the number of calories that it is burning. This is a particularly useful

▲ *Certain small dogs such as dachshunds are likely to venture underground, and tracking will reveal their location.*

feature if your dog was obese when you acquired it, and you are working to slim your pet down.

A fitness boost

Although it is popularly thought that all dogs in most rescue centres will have been neglected previously and so will be underweight, this is not necessarily the case. Dogs in rescue centres are often brought in as overweight, having been fed a diet of unsuitable food, and it then becomes very important to the dog's overall health that it is slimmed down again. Obese dogs suffer from typical issues such as *diabetes mellitus*, joint pain and heart disease.

Improving the situation, and prolonging your dog's life, depends on a two-pronged approach. One will be following the centre's advice on diet, and the second will be maintaining a suitable exercise regimen to burn off the surplus calories. This becomes much easier

◄ A tracker can serve to monitor your dog's level of activity, helping to indicate its fitness. Various options are available for this purpose.

once your dog can start exploring and running off the leash when you go out for walks. Being able to monitor its activity levels via a tracker is a vital part of this programme, enabling you to see the fitness of your dog improving over time. There is also the possibility of comparing your pet's level of activity with those of other dogs in your neighbourhood.

Practical usage

GPS units to track your dog are not costly, but you will need to sign up for an ongoing service that enables you to access the service as well. There are different plans on offer, so check these carefully, and choose the one that is most applicable to your needs. Some of the more expensive packages allow your dog to be tracked by more than one person, which can be useful if you travel and are not always at home. It means that your partner or a friend will be able to watch over your dog as well.

If you travel with your pet, even overseas, you should find that the GPS tracking system works in many other countries, so you may well find that you still benefit from the coverage. This can be the time when tracking is most important, when you are away from home with your pet walking in unfamiliar surroundings, as it is then easier for you to get separated. Your dog may get spooked, perhaps by the sound of shooting or thunder, and run off.

If you are unfortunate enough to lose your pet, these devices have a battery life which lasts typically between two and five days, making it possible to keep on your dog's trail for an adequate period to allow you to be reunited. It is probably worth investing in a spare battery, especially if you are travelling, so that you can keep the spare fully charged and swap them round when necessary. Tracker batteries are usually charged using a USB system, so you do not necessarily need to be able to connect with a mains supply.

▼ Monitoring can help to prevent the worry when a dog disappears, enabling you to be reunited quickly.

Toys for your dog

One of the best ways of developing the bond with your pet, both in the home and outside, is to invest in some suitable toys, although at first, the dog may not be especially interested in playing, needing to gain enthusiasm first. Do not be tempted to buy cheap plastic toys as these are easily ripped apart by sharp teeth and hard parts can be swallowed and lodge in your pet's stomach.

◄ Bright-coloured toys are recommended for use outdoors, where they will be highly visible.

There are a wide range of different toys to choose from, suitable for all dogs and designed in such a way that they will appeal to a dogs of different ages and types. If you have difficulty throwing a toy for your dog to chase, there are also aids to help in this regard. In fact, you are quite likely to end up requiring a toy basket where you can keep your pet's toys. What is especially interesting is that dogs do tend to end up with their own favourites, and this cannot be predicted.

Plush and chew toys

Young puppies particularly are drawn to plush (soft) toys, which are light, and so they can be cuddled, carried around, and even chewed. Toys of this type do not give so much opportunity to interact with you, compared with many other styles, but you can still throw a soft toy over a short distance and your puppy will soon learn to go off and retrieve it. The problem with soft toys, however, is that as your dog gets bigger, it may also become more destructive, causing soft toys to split, with their fluffy contents likely to be spilt out over the floor. Clear this up so your dog will not get the material stuck in its teeth or swallow it.

A range of chew toys and chews are available, and these are particularly helpful for puppies that are teething, serving to ease the associated discomfort. Chewing can be beneficial in any event, helping to prevent a build-up of tartar on the teeth, which may be a cause of halitosis (bad breath) and contributes to gum inflammation and tooth loss.

Action toys

Tug toys serve as a rather more active form of chew toy, and are often favoured by stronger, more combative types of dogs, including Staffordshire bull terriers. Avoid letting things become too heated with this type of toy though; it may be a good idea to pause the game by dropping your side of the tug and throwing a ball for your dog to chase and retrieve instead.

There are also toys that you can obtain which bounce unpredictably, and many dogs enjoy chasing after these, and bringing them back so they can be thrown again. You just need to be careful that you do not start playing with this type of toy if there are people around!

▼ Tug toys are popular with young, strong dogs, but do not allow your pet to become aggressive in this situation.

◄ Many dogs are keen to chase after balls and will learn almost instinctively to bring the toy back with them so you can throw it again.

► Some toys will test your pet's intelligence. Here the dog needs to find the treat, and then slide the wooden cover across to reach it.

Special balls are marketed as dog toys, and these tend to be quite robust. They are also available in various sizes and colours. It can be useful to buy brightly coloured examples, and then if your pet loses interest and simply abandons the ball, you will have a better chance of being able to find it in the garden or elsewhere afterwards.

Learning to 'drop'

Most dogs enjoy chasing after a ball, and soon learn to bring it back to you to throw again. This provides a good opportunity to teach your pet to drop items. Give the instruction and don't forget to use the clicker to reinforce the fact that the dog has responded as required. If you do need to take the ball out of the dog's mouth, however, this is something that you will need to do carefully, partly because you cannot be sure that it won't snap at you.

You may therefore want to wear a pair of robust but flexible gardening gloves at this stage. Place your left hand over the snout, about midway down your dog's upper jaw, while using your other hand to prise down the lower jaw, so that the ball will fall out of its mouth on to the ground where you can retrieve it. Before long, when you say 'drop', you will find that your dog starts to do so automatically, and then hopefully in the future, if it picks up something that it should not have, it will drop it without a problem (For more advice on teaching your dog to 'drop', see page 167).

Stick to the canine versions

It is not a good idea to use a lightweight football, because although even small dogs love playing with these, steering them along with their jaws, the game is often short-lived. Sooner, rather than later, your dog's teeth are likely to puncture the ball, allowing the air to escape so it rapidly deflates.

Equally, many dogs enjoy playing with flying discs, but be sure to obtain the canine version of these popular toys. This is because those that are sold for human use tend to be made of harder material, and this could hurt your dog if it inadvertently gets hit by the disc.

◄ Many toys are multipurpose, serving either as a chew or something to chase and may be used a tug-toy as well.

Sporting possibilities

If you have a young and relatively fit dog, then you can start to build a bond further with your pet by participating in one of the growing number of canine sports that are on offer, such as agility tests, catching skills like Flyball and off-road racing such as Canicross. It may even be possible to compete together as part of a team, although you will probably need to start in a more modest way initially.

If you have a garden you can set up a fun obstacle course to see if your pet is interested in this sort of thing.

Agility courses

There are several different components in an agility course, ranging from poles, through which the dogs must weave, to jumps, tunnels and other items, even possibly a see-saw.

Competing in agility contests is quite demanding and it is not recommended that dogs under a year old start to train in agility. They can usually only participate in events after 18 months of age.

One of the great things about agility contests is that any dog can take part – whether pure-bred or not – and they are grouped according to size in the larger competitions. It has proved to be a popular spectator sport since being introduced for the first time during the 1970s at the famous Crufts Dog Show.

▲ *You don't need expensive equipment for sports training – you can teach your dog to weave initially with a row of canes, and then progress to poles.*

A dog needs to negotiate the course by going round in the correct order, and it must not miss out any poles or other obstacles, being guided around them in the correct sequence by its handler. You will therefore need to familiarize yourself with the layout of the course before the competition begins.

Its design is not standardized as such, and tests both you and your dog's observational skills, working together under pressure. Bribing with treats is not permitted, and it is simply a question of the dog and handler working together closely as a team to get around the course in a winning time with no faults.

Even if you do not actually want to compete at a top level, however, you can still join a local canine agility club and have great fun with your pet. You will be able to meet other people who share your interest in dogs, and it is a great opportunity for your dog to socialize too, as well as helping both of you to keep fit.

Co-ordination and catching skills

With flying discs being so popular for dogs as toys, it is perhaps not surprising that catching the discs has grown up into a competitive sport, although perhaps strangely, relatively few people participate in this type of event. Any dog can take part, but again fitness is a requisite.

◄ *A dog emerges from a tunnel which forms part of an agility course. This sporting activity helps to build trust between you and your pet.*

► *Special soft flying discs are produced for dogs, and these are often popular with individuals which have an athletic build.*

◄ Flyball tests both a dog's agility and its speed, as it needs to catch the ball and to be able to run fast as well.

You also need to practise your throwing skills, because there are points to be awarded for throwing the disc, as well as for the dog's ability to catch it. Difficult catches, when the dog manages to grab the disc successfully in mid-air with all four feet off the ground, will score highly. At bigger contests, the classes are often divided into long and short throwing, as well as freestyle.

When training your dog for events of this type, you will need a level and relatively soft surface. In the initial stages, you want to throw the disc so your pet can catch it easily, gaining an insight into what is required and build up its confidence. You can then start aiming the disc above the dog's head, so that it will need to turn to chase after the disc.

Before long, having understood what is required, your dog will soon begin to leap into the air to grab it. Small, agile dogs such as Jack Russell terriers can be very successful at catching these discs after a bit of practice, and collies are also often highly adept in this field.

Flyball is another competitive canine sport which relies in part on agility and has captured people's imaginations since it began during the 1970s in southern California. It has now become popular worldwide. Two teams of dogs race against each other, jumping over hurdles, with each individual then triggering the release of a ball at each end of the course which must be retrieved and carried back over the hurdles.

Again, Flyball is open to dogs of all types and sizes, with the jumps being set to accommodate the smallest member of the team. The contest is timed against the clock, and the results can be very close. Successful contestants need to be able to run fast, and retrieve well, in addition to being agile.

▼ A Canicross competition. Dogs and people run together, with the dog attached to its owner during the race.

MORE PHYSICAL OPTIONS

There are various other sporting competitions which dogs can take part in with their owners, but these are linked more closely to the physique of the dog. Canicross, for example, involves running with your dog over a set course which is entirely off road and features different types of terrain.

During this type of event , you will be wearing a special harness, which encourages the dog to pull ahead, while remaining attached to the person accompanying it by a belt. A strong physique and stamina are key attributes for success in canicross, and unsurprisingly perhaps, dogs of spitz ancestry, such as the Siberian husky, which were bred to pull sleds in the far north, often excel in this activity, although any dog – including mongrels – can take part and sometimes there may be more than one dog running together. Canicross is fast becoming a popular sport, which can be accessed at all levels, from a run in the countryside with friends to entering a serious compeition.

Canibiking is a variation on this theme, with the dog wearing a harness and being attached to a bike.

Feeding

It is important to provide your dog with a nutritious diet that is appropriate for its age, health status and activity level. Today, professional nutritionists provide feeds of a variety and quality that should satisfy any dog, packaged in forms convenient enough to suit any owner. Most dogs, especially when they are well-settled in their home, are very easy to feed, and are not at all fussy about their food.

Dogs are carnivores. Their digestive system is designed to cope with a meat diet. The dog's teeth are adapted to tear food into chunks that can be swallowed rather than to grind the food, and their stomachs can digest food in this stage.

Dogs have evolved from wolves that have a primarily meat-based diet. However, when meat is not available to them, wolves seek other types of food, such as plants and berries, and the dog is able to eat a diet that is mostly plant matter; but a complete

▼ *Most dogs will eat readily, but if your dog is nervous, it may be reluctant to do so. Always feed your pet in a quiet area of the home.*

absence of meat will lead to nutritional deficiencies. Today's vegetarian diets for dogs are formulated to take these needs into account. In addition, there are now dog foods made from dried insects as a source of protein rather than meat.

You may find, in the case of a dog that has been poorly nourished in the past, that you need to start off on one food, as advised by the centre, and then change this over time as its condition improves. Some dogs can also suffer badly with diarrhoea, which may be linked with their food. Keep your pet on a diet of white meat, such as chicken or turkey under these circumstances, rather than one containing beef, and use a

▲ *Your dog's food intake should reflect its life-stage and activity level.*

probiotic to help in populating the gut with beneficial bacteria. Once you have found a food that suits your pet, try to avoid changing it. A dog will not become bored eating the same food every day. Any unavoidable changes should only be made gradually.

Commercial feeds

Dog foods may be divided into several broad categories. For many years, the so-called 'wet' diets held the major part of the market. They are the canned foods seen on every supermarket shelf, although they are equally likely to be sold in pouches and trays today. Complete dry (or kibbled) feeds are increasingly popular. They need minimal preparation – if desired, they can simply be poured into a dog bowl and given to the dog. It is only very slightly more demanding to pour warm water on to moisten the feed, which tends to increase its palatability.

NUTRIENTS

The major nutrients, required in substantial quantities by every animal, include the following.
• Carbohydrates, which provide the body with energy, and in surplus will be converted into body fat.
• Fats, which are the most concentrated form of energy, producing more than twice as much energy, weight for weight, than carbohydrates, and which will also convert to body fats if supplied in excess.
• Proteins, which essentially provide the body-building elements in the diet.

The minor nutrients include the vitamins, minerals and trace elements, which although critical to the animal's health, are required in comparatively small amounts.

The vitamins are usually divided into two groups:
• Fat-soluble: vitamins A, D, E and K.
• Water-soluble: the B complex vitamins and vitamin C.

Semi-moist foods are not widely recommended by veterinary surgeons, nor favoured by many owners. Their unhealthy reputation stems from the fact they tend to contain more than their share of unhealthy additives such as sugar.

Raw foods

These have become more popular over recent years, and as their name suggests, the ingredients are offered without being cooked. There is a risk,

► *Most dogs love bones, but small, fragile bones as in chicken carcasses are especially dangerous. Raw marrow bones (as shown) can spread bacterial infections. Buy prepared ones, which are clean, and have a filling for the dog to eat.*

however, that dogs could be receiving a higher load of potential bacteria which, especially for a dog whose immune system may not be in the best of health, is not to be recommended. The risks of transmitting zoonotic diseases such as salmonellosis and campylobacteriosis to you and your family are also much higher than with cooked food, even though human-grade ingredients are being used.

One feature of modern formulated dog foods is that they will contain adequate minor nutrients, which did not always happen in the meat and biscuit days. The outcome is that there is rarely any need for the proprietary feed supplements that are still widely advertised. Calcium, for instance, may have been lacking in some traditional diets, and a

bonemeal supplement often used to be recommended. Today this is not often necessary. Speak with your local vet for further information about this.

▼ *If you have more than one dog, always feed them separately. Mealtimes can develop into a serious flashpoint between individuals.*

Reviewing your dog's diet

It may be necessary to provide a special diet in some cases, for younger or ageing dogs, and also to support dogs with a long-standing illness. Even so, it is not a good idea to change your dog's food suddenly – less so because this may cause a loss of appetite, but because it is more likely to result in diarrhoea. Loss of appetite and an upset stomach are all causes of concern that need urgent attention.

After your dog has been with you for a certain amount of time you may be tempted to alter their diet.

Special diets

You obviously need to be particularly careful in the case of dogs that suffer from digestive-related complaints, such as colitis or indeed pancreatitis, where a special diet is essential to keep this condition stabilized, as well as ensuring your pet does not become overweight. Chronic (meaning 'long-standing') kidney disease is another illness where food can have a significant overall influence on your dog's condition. Special renal diets for kidney sufferers are available, which have a lower protein component than

▼ *A variety of special diets are now available for older dogs, helping to meet their specific nutritional requirements.*

normal dog food. In all these cases, any changes to the diet should be made only based on veterinary advice. There is no need to worry that your dog may get bored with its food, being offered the same every day. Dogs do not suffer boredom with food in the way that we would, and prepared foods on the market today are carefully formulated to ensure that they meet your dog's nutritional requirements.

Life-stage diets are widely available today, and these have been formulated to meet the changing nutritional requirements of your dog as it grows older. If you started off with a puppy who was being fed on a puppy food, then you will need to switch across to an adult food from about a year old, depending partly on the eventual size of your dog.

Equally, if you took on an older individual, you would probably need

to switch to a food for senior dogs, typically at seven to eight years of age, that will be more suited to its needs. These senior dog foods (see page 98) are specially formulated partly to prevent your pet putting on weight when its level of activity is naturally slowing down.

Loss of appetite

As a guide, the smallest dogs like Chihuahuas are far more likely to be fussy eaters than their bigger counterparts. This can be a behavioural problem, sometimes reflecting the fact that the dog does not feel secure in its surroundings. Always feed a newcomer in a quiet spot in the home, leaving it there to eat at its own speed. Most dogs, however, will

▼ *Feeding your dog regularly in the same place and at the same times will encourage your pet to eat without problems.*

instinctively gulp down their food. This is quite normal behaviour.

It is usual to feed a dog in the kitchen, but this can be quite a busy thoroughfare, especially in the morning, with people coming and going. It may be better to wait until the home is quieter, or to feed your dog elsewhere. Always be careful with food, however, because some dogs can become unexpectedly possessive around their food bowl, displaying uncharacteristic aggression, even if they do not eat the contents straight away (see page 117).

Should your dog refuse its food, there can be several reasons, not overlooking the fact that this can be an early sign of illness. Watch how your dog behaves – if it rushes up to its food, and then picks some up in its mouth, before dropping most of it again, this can indicate dental pain, especially in an older dog.

Dogs that are naturally sensitive eaters can be put off their food by the way that it is presented. Generally, dogs prefer wet food to dry food, but offering a portion of food straight out of the refrigerator is likely to be off-putting, because it is cold. Allow the portion of food to warm up, as this will make it more palatable to your pet.

Gut health

When changing the diet of your dog, it can help to smooth the transition by mixing the two foods together, gradually increasing the amount of the new food on offer over a few weeks. This should avoid not just the risk of diarrhoea, but also the problem of flatulence, which can be an issue, especially for flat-faced (or brachycephalic) breeds like French bulldogs.

There are several causes of flatulence, some of which can again be indicative of an underlying health issue, but also, dogs with this profile swallow a lot of air when eating their food quickly because of their facial shape. It can therefore help simply to

► *Flatulence can be a problem associated with dogs which have flattened faces. Altering your pet's diet may help, encouraging it to eat more slowly using a food tray, and traditionally, special canine garlic tablets have also been used. Probiotics may help too, especially after a course of antibiotics.*

acquire a special food container which will make it harder for your pet to gulp down its food so quickly. Feeders of this type contain ridges which mean that it may prolong your pet's feeding time ten-fold. They are suitable for all types of food and need carefully scrubbing clean.

Another way of helping to improve your dog's digestive health is to use a probiotic. There are various brands on the market, offering different types of beneficial bacteria that help to stabilize the digestive microflora that are present in your dog's intestinal tract. These products are usually flavoured, and therefore quite palatable. A probiotic is particularly useful if your dog has recently had to be on a long-standing course of antibiotic therapy, which is likely to have impacted adversely on the numbers of these helpful bacteria, or to aid recovery from a digestive upset.

Weight and obesity

Alongside consideration of the type of food that you are offering, it is also very important to be aware of your dog's weight. Just as with people, so the number of dogs that are overweight or even obese has grown dramatically over recent years. You must monitor your pet's weight regularly, and take action to help it to lose weight if necessary before any lasting harm is done.

There are several reasons for obesity in dogs, including the excessive use of treats and over-feeding generally, combined with a lack of exercise, but an underlying cause is simply the fact that many owners do not actually spot that their pet is putting on weight until the situation is well-advanced, by which stage, it becomes significantly harder to address.

The impact of obesity in dogs is like that in people. Perhaps most marked, however, is that this can place additional stress on the joints, restricting the dog's mobility. It is very easy to get into the start of a downward spiral as a result, with your pet then becoming less active and putting on more weight unless steps are taken to address the situation.

▼ *Regular weight monitoring is vital for all dogs, allowing you to address increasing weight gain before it becomes a serious issue.*

▲ *Certain types of dogs are more vulnerable to obesity than others. The risk of the problem increases as they age.*

Your dog may even be overweight when you first acquired it, and in need of losing some pounds. The rescue centre is likely to have devised a targeted weight loss plan for your pet, and it is very important to stick to these recommendations. In any event, you need to monitor your pet's weight from the outset.

The importance of monitoring

It may be possible to persuade your dog to stand (or even sit) with its body weight on a pair of bathroom scales. This will make it easy to obtain a figure. Always aim to weigh your dog first thing in the morning, before it has eaten, so you can get the most accurate figure before it has been fed. You should then record this figure in a diary, repeating this routine roughly every two weeks. If your dog is reluctant to co-operate, then you can stand on the scales yourself, holding your dog, and subsequently subtract your weight from the overall figure.

In terms of determining what your pet should weigh, this will be easier if your dog is a pure-bred. All you need to do is to find the national kennel club site online, and then you will be able to track down the ideal weight of your dog from the show standard for that breed.

If you have a cross-bred or a mongrel, however, this will not be so easy, but ask your vet for an approximate weight. There are also various signs that you can use to indicate whether your pet is overweight. The most obvious indicator is if the ribs have become hidden under a covering of fat, and are hard to feel when you stroke your pet. The abdomen is likely to be sagging downwards, and the dog's waist has disappeared as well, with the surrounding area across the back having expanded in width.

These visual signs will be most apparent in short-coated dogs, but you may note behavioural signs as well, with the dog being less active than was the case beforehand. One thing to be particularly aware of is that after neutering, dogs are very

▲ *Severe obesity affects a dog's entire appearance, imposes more weight on its joints and can contribute to a host of ailments.*

▲ *Thieving of kitchen counter tops or being fed regularly at mealtimes by members of the family can both contribute to cases of obesity.*

inclined to put on weight. Cutting back on food at this stage will probably be necessary.

Taking action

There are special slimming foods that you can purchase, to help your dog to lose weight. These have relatively few calories and low fat but will make your dog feel full. There is typically a high level of protein in them as well, to preserve muscle through this period, with supplements in terms of vitamins, minerals and similar key nutritional components included too, all designed at the appropriate levels.

It is especially important to cut down drastically on treats if you use them – or better still, replace them entirely with healthier options such as the occasional small piece of carrot. You also need to start getting your dog exercising more, in moderation to begin with, and gradually building this up as its level of fitness improves. You will also need to consider any other underlying health issues that your

dog may have, such as joint or heart ailments, when planning out the exercise schedule.

You can start off in a moderate way in your garden perhaps, throwing a ball or flying disc for your dog to run after and bring back to you. It doesn't necessarily mean that you need to take your dog for longer walks – particularly once your pet is trained to chase after balls or other toys and bring them back to you. By so doing, your dog will

▼ *If you take on an obese dog, the rescue centre will work with you on a plan to slim down your new pet, through diet and exercise.*

effectively be covering twice the distance that you are under these circumstances, doubling the level of exercise that it will be receiving when out on a walk.

Activities such as agility work can be very useful to control the weight of younger dogs, once they have built up a level of fitness. In the case of older or more infirm dogs, hydrotherapy (see page 110) can help to provide a solution.

Grooming your dog

Having a dog is something that, hopefully, everyone in the family will be enthusiastic about and from a practical point of view it is important that the dog learns to trust and respond to all members of the household. However, nervous dogs may react badly at first to direct physical contact which is necessary for bathing, grooming and routine health checks, such as dental hygiene.

Some rescue dogs, especially those that have had a tough start in life, may instinctively tend to bond to a greater extent with one person, being suspicious with other people. This can often happen rather by default, as the dog responds better to one person, who then assumes greater responsibility for its care.

The situation is likely to be worse in the case of a dog which was mistreated in its past and has gained a particular lack of trust towards men for example. Hopefully, this is something which you will have been made aware of from the outset, however, and can work to counter effectively over time.

Much of this can be achieved with patience, as you develop a daily routine at home with your pet. Different members of the household should feed the dog, rather than just one person, and be involved in exercising the dog and taking in part in other aspects of its care.

Routine grooming

Things can be rather difficult when direct contact for grooming purposes is necessary, especially if the dog is not used to this experience anyway. A dog that is instinctively nervous under these circumstances needs careful handling and reassurance, because otherwise, it is likely to be very uncooperative. It will try wriggling to break free, and in some cases, it may even start growling and snapping to escape being held.

▲ *The amount of grooming that a dog requires is very variable. Greyhound-type dogs have a thin coat and need relatively little in terms of coat care.*

The amount of grooming required depends on your dog's coat, as clearly longhaired dogs need more regular grooming than their short-coated counterparts. It is important to keep up grooming of longhaired dogs, because otherwise, if the coat becomes badly matted, then grooming out these mats is likely to be painful for your dog, making it resent the process even more.

You may be able to obtain a detangling comb, the teeth of which rotate. This serves to break down areas where the hair has become tangled, without pulling at it, thereby making the grooming process more comfortable for your dog. Otherwise, the only way to remove matted areas from the coat will be to cut them out carefully, with blunt-ended scissors.

In the early stages, however, try to concentrate on stroking your pet, and picking up its front paws gently as part of this routine. Lift the ears too, when stroking the head, and persuade your dog that it has nothing to be fearful of, by talking reassuringly in a quiet voice at the same time.

▼ *Dogs moult more heavily in the spring, shedding their thicker winter coat, and different grooming tools may assist then.*

▼ *Dogs that are not used to being groomed, or have found it painful in the past, can be nervous about this experience.*

◄ Some dogs are instinctively happier having a bath than others, but there are various steps that you can take to pacify a nervous individual during the process.

► Being able to open your dog's mouth is important for various reasons, but you need to be very careful to ensure that you will not be bitten.

Giving your pet a bath

One specific aspect of life which your dog may not have experienced to any extent before is having a bath, and this can be frightening experience for it at first. It is not a good idea to use your own bath – not just on grounds of hygiene, but also because your dog could damage the surface with its claws.

Instead, a plastic baby bath can be very useful for this purpose, also because it allows you to bathe your dog outside, where it will not matter if a lot of splashing occurs. Dogs generally will require a bath every three to four months, when their characteristic odour starts to become strong, although this depends rather on the individual.

When you are bathing your dog, make sure that everything is organized in advance, and that your chosen doggy shampoo is to hand. You also need to have a plastic jug or something similar that can be used for baling water. Part-fill the bath with warm (not hot) water, and then lift your dog carefully into it. You only need the water to come up halfway to the top of your dog's legs, partly as this will make your pet less inclined to struggle, although you will probably need another member of your household to hold your dog, so it does not jump out of the water.

Then use the baling jug, gently pour the water over the dog's back, starting at the hindquarters and moving forwards. Once you have reached the neck, start shampooing the coat. Dogs frequently dislike having water on their heads, and there is a real risk that the shampoo may enter your pet's eye and sting, so try to avoid this area.

It is then a matter of rinsing the shampoo thoroughly out of the coat, and letting your dog step out of the bath. It is probably best to stand back at this point as your pet will shake itself vigorously to remove much of the residual water from its coat. Most dogs do not appreciate hairdryers, so simply towel-dry your pet after it has shaken itself, and keep it warm indoors, allowing it to dry off thoroughly here.

There are times of course, especially with wire-coated dogs, where they will need to visit a professional grooming parlour, to keep them looking at their best. They can be bathed at the same time, and this service can be useful if your dog is reluctant to have a bath at home.

Opening your dog's mouth

It can be much harder to win the confidence of a nervous dog, so you can open its mouth and inspect or even clean its teeth. Ideally, you want to do this when your pet is tired, as it may be less resistant to the idea. Start by supporting the lower jaw with one hand, before gently lifting the upper lip, and see how your dog reacts.

You need to get to a stage where you can part the jaws, without fear of being bitten. This will allow you to retrieve items that your dog has picked up, which could be harmful to it if swallowed. You will ideally need someone who can hold your dog steady and reassure it during this period.

If you are right-handed, the safest way to open the jaws is to place your left hand over the bridge of the nose, to steady the upper jaw, and then to raise the head slightly, and prise down the lower jaw.

Clearly, if your dog needs regular medication in the form of tablets right from the outset, so you have had no chance to bond, a different approach may be needed. There are special treats that you can acquire, designed so that you can slip a tablet inside and hopefully, your dog will not notice it when it is offered in this way! You mould the treat around the pill to hold it in place, after inserting it. If your dog is diabetic, however, you will need to check that this type of treat can be used safely for your pet.

Your dog and holidays

As time passes, and your dog settles into life with you, there will come the point where you have to decide what to do with your pet where holidays are concerned. Dog owners who wish to take a holiday have three options: find alternative care for their dog, take the dog with them, or have a vacation at home. Each option takes some time to organize.

When considering which option to take, it is very important to ensure that your dog will not become traumatized, especially in these early months with you.

Taking your dog with you

This may appear to be the most obvious solution although it may not be feasible, even if you are holidaying domestically. It may also not be the best option for a nervous or infirm individual, because of the travelling involved.

While your dog could travel with you in your vehicle, it will not be safe to leave it alone here when you are parked up and heading to a restaurant to eat, where dogs are not welcomed. They can die literally in minutes in the confines of a locked vehicle, as the temperature within can rapidly rise to a fatal level.

If you are renting somewhere to stay, where dogs are permitted, your pet may suffer badly from stress when left in strange surroundings on its own, damaging or soiling its surroundings, or barking constantly and disturbing other guests nearby. Exercising your pet in unfamiliar surroundings may be an issue too, because of the risk that your dog might run off and disappear.

Much obviously depends on the individual, but overall, you will almost inevitably have to plan your holiday carefully around your dog's needs if you decide to take this option. On the other hand, it does mean that

you will have more opportunity to bond together and travelling with you may help to bolster your pet's confidence.

When planning the journey to your destination, factor in extra time to allow your dog a comfort stop and a chance to stretch its legs. Take familiar items with you, such as the dog's bed and toys, to ensure your pet's comfort and to help it settle into its new surroundings.

Home-sitting

Having someone coming to stay in your home and take care of your dog (and any other pets) while you are away is now an increasingly popular option. But it is important to do your research and find a reputable company offering this type of service. You should also check that this will not affect your home insurance. Home-sitting has the major

▲ When you go away it does not mean that your dog will have to go back into kennels. You may be able to arrange for someone to stay and look after your pet.

advantage that your dog will not have to go into kennels while you are away, which is particularly helpful for a nervous dog, although it will not be used to the person looking after it. Nevertheless, most home-sitters

▼ Canvas or fabric portable kennels are easy to transport and provide a safe haven for your dog on holiday.

► *Try not to acquire your pet if you are going away soon afterwards. This will be very disorientating for the dog if it then must be returned to boarding kennels, after just settling in with you.*

have extensive experience with dogs, and will soon win your pet's confidence, so there should not be any major cause for concern. Ensure that the person moving in is insured, licensed by appropriate authorities, and has had a police check. Always ask for references and follow these up. It goes without saying that you will need to leave detailed instructions about your pet's routine and feeding requirements.

You may have a friend who will take your dog into their home and look after it while you are away. However, this will be more traumatic for your dog than staying in familiar surroundings, as it has to settle in a new environment again – albeit only on a temporary basis – and old habits, such as separation anxiety, may re-emerge and cause problems.

Boarding kennels

If you do want to try a boarding kennel, try to arrange everything as early as possible. This means that you should then have less difficulty finding somewhere local with a vacancy on the dates that you need.

Always make sure that you visit the kennels first, before confirming any booking, and ask for a recommendation from the rescue centre too. They are likely to have contacts with kennels in the local area that they may also use on occasions.

Kennels will expect vaccinations to be up-to-date, and most insist that

dogs are vaccinated against kennel cough. Ensure this is all in order several weeks before your holiday, especially as some dogs can feel a little under the weather for a short period after a vaccination. It is a good idea to book your dog into the chosen kennel for a day, a few weeks before your holiday, to see if it settles. This will give you peace of mind too.

Festive holidays

Some holiday periods, such as Christmas, might be taken at home, often in the company of friends and relatives. Many dogs enjoy the bustle and excitement of these events, but some do not. Provide your dog with a quiet place that it can retreat to if it wishes. Make sure guests understand that some food items, such as chocolate, Christmas cake and alcohol, are toxic to dogs and should be placed out of reach and not offered as treats.

Some holiday celebrations involve noise. Fireworks are not only heard on Bonfire Night or Independence Day, but also as part of New Year parties and Diwali celebrations. These, and Christmas crackers, can terrify noise-shy dogs. If you suspect that loud noises may be part of your

holiday celebrations, shut your dog away somewhere safe and comfortable and keep the curtains drawn.

Whichever choice you make for your holiday, check that your dog has the required identification on its collar and that its microchip records are current. If your dog gets lost or is startled and runs off, these are essential elements to reunite owners with their dogs.

▼ *If you have no option but to send your pet to kennels, see if you can provide a favourite toy and a towel with the scent of home.*

Issues with ageing

Dogs today are generally living longer than at any stage in the past, although their lifespan tends to be influenced by their size. Small dogs live longer than their bigger relatives, with a life expectancy today that can extend well into their teens. On the other hand, a large dog may only live for a decade or less. Specialist diets and the right supplements are available to allow the older dog to continue enjoying life.

When taking on a rescue dog of course, it is often impossible to get a reliable insight into the dog's age. There are clues that can give some insight, most noticeably greying of the fur around the muzzle and eyes, although these changes can be more pronounced in some cases than others. If your dog has led a hard life before you acquired it, then it may appear older than is the case, as reflected by wear on its teeth, for example.

It is now possible to ensure your pet has a good quality of life as it grows older, thanks to advances in our understanding of the require-ments of older dogs. Firstly, in terms of feeding, it will be a good idea to

switch your pet to a senior diet, probably once it is about seven years old, or based on veterinary advice, if you are uncertain of your pet's age.

These foods are now widely available, and you are likely to find one within most dog food ranges. The ingredients are geared to the nutritional requirements of older dogs, so they include a higher level of protein, to maintain your pet's muscle tone, a moderate level of fat, and a reduction in the number of calories, compared with the food that your dog would probably have been eating previously.

Dietary changes

The lower calorific value of senior foods reflects the fall-off in energy levels of older dogs, with the aim being to prevent unwanted weight gain at this stage in life. It can be

▲ *As dogs grow older, so their exercise needs are likely to change, particularly if they have underlying health issues.*

much harder to achieve weight loss in a senior dog anyway, as it will not be so energetic, especially if your pet is suffering from any disability that may compromise its level of activity.

Dogs can suffer a degree of loss of cognitive function as they grow older, and with the aim of minimizing this problem, some senior foods are now incorporating higher levels of antioxidants. A type of oil known as MCT (which stands for 'medium-chain triglycerides') is being used for this purpose and has the benefit of being relatively easy for your dog to digest. It derives from either palm kernel or coconut oil and is also believed to help with regulating the dog's appetite and may therefore have weight loss benefits as well.

As your dog ages, so too will its joints, and it is now common to find

▼ *Adjusting your pet's diet should help it to stay livelier and more active as it ages, even though its coat becomes greyer.*

► *As a result of past injuries or joint deformities, some dogs may need more support, helping them to move around in later life.*

▼ *Older dogs will benefit from more regular veterinary check-ups, about every six months, enabling any issues to be detected earlier.*

ingredients like glucosamine in senior dog foods, that will help to minimize arthritic pain. As they age, a combination of reduced activity and a loss of muscle tone can also make older dogs more prone to constipation, and so senior foods usually contain a higher level of fibre to reduce this possibility.

It is not uncommon for senior dogs to suffer problems with major organs in the body. Special foods to mitigate issues such as heart disease may be advised by vets, along with medication as appropriate. These typically contain a lower level of sodium than normal and may have other beneficial ingredients such as essential Omega-3 fatty acids to assist cardiac function.

It will be worth discussing with your vet whether it will be better to switch to one of these more specialist diets (which can usually be acquired by mail order if required) rather than a more general senior food. A dog's kidney function also declines with age, and once again, the use of a carefully formulated prescription food can be advantageous in certain cases.

The role of supplements

There are also various supplements available that can be useful, helping to protect liver function for example, although you will not require a general vitamin and mineral supplement in most cases, because adequate levels will be present within the dog's food, assuming you are using a commercially prepared food. Obviously, a general-purpose supplement is much more likely to be important if you are feeding a home-prepared diet of any type; so check with your vet about what may be necessary.

A wide range of joint supplements to help your dog keep moving as freely as possible, are now available. These feature components such as glucosamine, chondroitin, and green-lipped mussel extract. The good news is that these can be given over a long period of time, without harmful side-effects. Nevertheless, it will be worth asking your vet about whether you should be giving your pet a supplement of this type.

Joint supplements can help to maintain the cartilage in a relatively healthy state in your pet's old age, as

▼ *Dogs become less active in old age, sometimes partly due to painful joints. Joint supplements can be beneficial.*

◄ *Less flexibility in old age means that dogs tend to prefer to lie on a canine duvet, rather than using a conventional dog bed.*

on work surfaces, as they will encounter difficulty and pain standing up on their hind legs. You may notice that your dog is avoiding various areas of your home, if the floor here is slippery, as it may be having difficulty in keeping its balance. Ideally, add rugs, which your pet will find easier to walk across.

When your dog is lying down, you may spot that it seems to be licking its legs more than usual. By behaving in this way, it is trying to soothe the pain emanating from its joints.

Based on your vet's advice, it is important that you still encourage your dog to exercise, but in a gentle fashion, mainly by walking. Do not encourage it to sprint after a ball though, even if it is keen to do so. Something that can be very useful in such cases however, because it supports the weight of the joints, thereby easing the pain, are regular hydrotherapy sessions (see below and pages 110–11).

well as ensuring that the joint fluid will make movement as easy as possible. They can also have an anti-inflammatory action, which is very important when a dog's joints are painful because of arthritis.

Coping with arthritis

Products to aid arthritic dogs are available in different forms, as tablets and capsules, as well as liquid supplements. Senior dog foods also incorporate ingredients of this type. Although these options can help, they do not provide a cure for arthritis, and so it is important to lift and handle an older dog with particular care, because its joints may still be painful. In severe cases, pain-killers from your vet may be required.

In cases of arthritis, your dog's hind leg muscles are likely to become weaker, and this can affect its lifestyle and behaviour, as these muscles naturally power its movements, when running for example. You are likely to notice differences in its lifestyle, even around the home.

Lifestyle changes

An aging dog will tend to sleep more on the floor, stretched out here rather than being curled up as was the case when it was younger. It will not move so fast or be as agile. Whereas in the past, it would leap enthusiastically into the back of the car to go out for a walk, now it will be reluctant to do so, and is likely to need a ramp to walk up here instead.

Arthritic dogs are not keen to climb stairs and will tend to avoid leaping up on to the sofa. They will also be less inclined to steal food left

◄ *One of the best ways to assist elderly dogs to maintain their muscular strength while minimizing joint pain is by means of regular hydrotherapy sessions. Your veterinary practice is likely to be aware of where there are facilities of this type in your area and can advise you accordingly.*

▲ *When stroking your pet, be aware of any unexpected swellings. This could indicate skin tumours or even ticks.*

▲ *Older dogs are less active and more vulnerable to feeling cold, so that they can often benefit from wearing a coat when out for a walk.*

As your dog gets older, so it is increasingly important to monitor its weight, and especially if your pet is suffering from arthritis because the additional weight will exert even more pressure on the joints. Be prepared to slim your dog down at this stage as required, which will also be essential if it has any other underlying conditions, such as heart disease, where again the extra weight will be a burden.

Be observant

If you notice any changes in your dog's behaviour when you are out walking, it will be worthwhile arranging a veterinary check-up. A slight cough after exercise can be a sign of a weakened heart valve, which may have been present for many years, but is now only giving rise to symptoms. You are also likely to notice that your dog will sleep more than it has done in the past.

Should you normally go for a walk with your dog in a park where there are many other dogs, try to pick a quiet time of day if possible, so that it will not become stressed with other younger dogs running around and coming up to it. In the past, it may have been happy to run around as part of a group, but the likelihood is

that it will prefer just to amble along now, without being challenged at all.

Always watch how your dog reacts to going for a walk, and when the weather is cold, you may need to fit your pet with a jumper, and possibly a coat as well, depending partly on the weather. This is likely to be essential for dogs like greyhounds that only have a thin top-coat of fur and little body fat, so they are not well-insulated against the cold. There are various designs that you can obtain, but make sure it is the right

▶ *The senses of older dogs become less acute, and they are likely not to be able to see or hear as well as when they were younger. This can lead to changes in behaviour, with your dog being disturbed unexpectedly by noise. Handling may become more difficult too if your pet's joints are painful.*

size for your dog, and that you can fit it easily, without it being painful for your pet.

Old dogs can become rather confused in their later years, even if they are living in familiar surroundings. Signs of this issue are likely to be most evident at night, and you will hear your dog moving around, barking, and sounding distressed. It may soil in the home at this stage as well. This breakdown in cognitive function has been likened to Alzheimer's disease in people, and there are similarities. Medication may help, but very sadly, this is a sign that your pet is finally reaching the end of the road, as you cannot turn back the clock.

Coping with disabilities

It may be that your dog's previous lifestyle has left it with a variable degree of disability. Collisions with vehicles, physical abuse or past untreated injuries are all examples of things that could have left a lasting permanent legacy on your new pet's health. While these issues may seem daunting at first, the rescue centre will offer plenty of support to help you accommodate your dog's healthcare needs.

The period during which you initially became acquainted will have provided you with a clear insight into the specific degree of disability that your dog is suffering. Every case is individual, and clearly, it is vital to discuss any particular care that your dog requires with rescue centre staff, so that you know what is involved, and the prognosis going forwards. You may also need to adapt things at home, to take account of your new pet's capabilities.

Back issues

Disc problems are not uncommon in smaller dogs. A 'slipped' intervertebral disc which causes paralysis of the hind limbs requires rest, so an affected individual will need to be kept quiet, and even hopefully after recovery, the risk of a recurrence remains. This is a relatively common issue, particularly in dachshunds and Pekingese, and may result from an old injury.

Under normal circumstances, these discs lie between the

◀ *Dogs can suffer disabilities as the result of an injury or accident, although the physique of some dogs such as those with long bodies can make them more vulnerable too.*

vertebrae, acting rather as shock absorbers. When a so-called 'slipped' disc occurs, it pings upwards, causing pressure on the spinal cord above. This is very painful in all cases, because of the nerve fibres located here. The actual symptoms are influenced to some extent by where in the spinal cord the disc has prolapsed. Problems in terms of walking and weakness of the hind limbs are usual.

With a dog known to have suffered from an injury of this type, it is therefore recommended to fit a stair gate (as sold for children), to prevent your pet from attempting to climb the stairs. You should also aim

to deter it from jumping up onto any chairs. Always make a point of picking up your dog carefully if you want it to sit with you, rather than asking it to leap up alongside you.

Useful equipment

Lift your dog into a car as well, and in the case of a larger individual with a history of back problems, obtain a special ramp that it can walk up into the back of your vehicle, rather than having to scramble up by itself. Dogs at risk should always be walked on a harness, rather than by a leash attached to a collar, as this can increase pressure in the vulnerable neck area.

◀ *Individuals that are at risk from disc problems should be discouraged from using stairs. A stair guard is recommended for this purpose.*

▶ *Special adjustable indoor walkways are available to help your dog get up and down off a chair.*

▶ A ramp is invaluable in helping an older, larger dog to move in and out of a vehicle easily, without having to be lifted in. You can soon train your pet to walk up and down here on its leash.

There is other equipment that can be useful too. Painful joints of any kind will cause a dog to suffer from discomfort, often to the extent that it may feel unable to lie down easily, especially if it has to curl up to fit into a relatively small bed. As a result, the bed will remain unused, and your dog may choose to lie on the floor instead, even though this will feel relatively hard.

What will be required therefore is a special orthopaedic mattress, which will give good support to your dog's limbs. These are available in different sizes, and have special foam within them, that provides gentle support. It may well be a good idea to purchase one for use in the home, and another that can be incorporated into the area of the car where your dog travels, to make the journey more comfortable.

It is also important to check the covering on the mattress, as with all dog beds. This needs to be easily removable, and washable, since particularly if used in a car, the bed is soon likely to become very muddy. Some designs have additional features that can be beneficial, such as a rubberized backing to make them more stable.

Incontinence issues

Should you have a dog that suffers from incontinence, then you may need to make additional adjustments in your home. It helps to have the home designed so that even if you have carpeting in some rooms, you can use somewhere with a moppable floor, in the kitchen perhaps, to locate your pet's bed. There are also some medications now that may help older dogs.

The other thing to bear in mind, especially if your dog has a long coat, is that its fur may end up being soiled on occasions, so that regular trimming of the fur and bathing are likely to be required. This will ensure that your pet does not have an unpleasant odour, and it will also lessen the risk of fly strike, which is a significant risk in warm weather. Blowflies may otherwise be attracted to the soiled areas of fur in the coat, laying their eggs here, which hatch rapidly into maggots. These in turn will bore into the skin, and release potentially deadly toxins into the dog's blood stream. Rapid veterinary treatment can be needed to save its life, with the maggots having to be removed without delay.

▼ A suitable mattress which can also fit into the back of the car will make it more comfortable for your dog when travelling.

First aid for your dog

An often-overlooked reason for concentrating on training is that it will help to protect your dog from injury or accidents. If your dog returns to you when called for example, you can stop it running into possible danger, such as an advancing vehicle. Even so, accidents still do happen and you may need to give emergency first aid to your pet, before you can seek veterinary advice.

If your dog is conscious after a serious accident, bear in mind that it is very likely to be in considerable pain as well as in shock. This means that it will be far more likely to bite you than would normally be the case, so extra care will be necessary when handling your injured pet.

Artificial respiration

If you suspect that your dog has stopped breathing, then immediate intervention on your part will be required. First of all look carefully at your pet's chest, to see if you can spot this part of the body moving up and down. This may not be so easy to see in a long-coated dog, compared with a sleek, smooth-coated individual.

Check there is no mucus or blood blocking the nostrils, and nothing lodged at the back of the throat that could obstruct the airways and may be interfering with your pet's breathing. Otherwise, any obstruction here will need to be carefully removed, taking particular care when you open your dog's mouth to avoid being bitten.

If you cannot detect your dog breathing again, then keep its mouth closed with your hands, and blow gently up the nostrils. You will then see the chest expand, as the air enters the lungs. Aim to keep the lungs inflated for a count of three, before letting the air out again. Continue in this rhythm every 5–10 seconds.

◀ Make sure that you can find your pet's heartbeat easily, in case you have to do so in an emergency situation. You can practice this simply when your dog is relaxed and lying down on its right-hand side.

You will probably also need to check for a heartbeat. The best way to locate the area for this purpose is to flex the elbow on the left-hand side of the body, with your dog lying on its right. At the point of the elbow, where it lies over the body, gentle pressure here between the ribs should enable you to pick up the heartbeat using the tips of your fingers.

It is worth experimenting so that you can find the heartbeat easily, which will give you more confidence in an emergency. Should there be no detectable beat, you will need to compress this area up and down, alternating this with the breathing routine every 15–20 seconds.

Sadly, if there is no detectable heartbeat within about four minutes, the chances are that the heart will not restart. On the other hand, if you can detect a heartbeat, continue giving artificial respiration for 20 minutes or so, in the hope of triggering your dog to commence breathing independently again.

Bleeding

The amount of blood loss will depend on the type of injury and the part of the body affected. Some injuries can result in severe internal haemorrhaging into the chest or abdomen, and the signs may not be apparent, in terms of any significant external blood loss. This is one reason why a dog should always be checked over as soon as possible afterwards by a vet, if it has been in a road traffic collision for example. A loss of pink colouration to the gums can be an indication of internal haemorrhaging, but it is also a sign of shock.

In cases where blood loss is evident, the first thing to do is to wrap the affected area, and apply pressure by tying the bandage in place, which will hopefully help to stem the blood flow. You may also need to create a temporary muzzle, by looping a belt for example over the dog's jaws, so that it does not try to bite you. It will then be a question of seeking veterinary assistance without delay, contacting a practice nearest to

▲ *To treat a wound, keep pressure on the wound to minimize any blood loss. Apply a bandage to cover it, using a non-stick dressing and a soft cotton bandage.*

▲ *In an emergency, masking tape or adhesive tape may be used instead of elastoplast to hold the dressing in place. Take the adhesive bandage 3cm (1in) up the fur to stop it slipping off.*

where you are, if you are some distance away from your regular vet.

Bites and stings

Dogs are often inclined to snap at flying insects, including bees and wasps without appreciating the potential danger if they catch one in their mouth.

The risk of this occurring depends to some extent where you live, with the risk being highest in tropical areas, where there are also more venomous snakes and invertebrates.

▼ *It will be impossible to prevent your dog from snapping at a flying insect and potentially getting stung.*

Yet even in temperate zones, the risk still applies, especially during the warmer months. A young dog will be most inclined to snap at any bees or wasps in the garden. If it catches one, and is stung at the back of the throat, then the tissue here will swell up, possibly blocking off the airway.

Seek veterinary advice immediately, and it will be helpful to know if a bee or wasp was the cause, because immediate home treatments differ, using a solution of bicarbonate of soda or vinegar respectively. An icepack can help with an external sting. Bach Flower Rescue Remedy can also be used as a complementary remedy in this situation too, while in terms of homeopathy, either Aconite 6C or 30C may be favoured.

Heat exhaustion

Some breeds of dog are more prone to heat exhaustion than others – Chow Chows and Bulldogs, for example, but other short-nosed breeds can also be affected.

The most common reason for heat exhaustion is human error. Dogs are too often left inside cars in summer without any thought. The

temperature inside a car in summer in even a temperate climate can kill a dog within minutes.

The signs of heat stress are obvious distress, heavy panting and an inability to breathe deeply enough, indicated by a half-strangled noise coming from the dog's throat. The dog's tongue looks swollen and blue.

Treat heat stroke as an immediate emergency, and do not attempt to take the dog to the vet until you have started to cool it down.

▼ *Plenty of cool (not cold) water and shade is the first-aid treatment for heat exhaustion. A wet towel will help to cool the dog down.*

Natural treatments for chronic pain

While in certain cases, actual pain relief in the form of medication prescribed by a vet may be required, there are often other things that you can do to help your dog to feel more comfortable. Always bear in mind, however, that if a dog is in pain, it may react aggressively when being handled, so take extra care if you need to pick your pet up and avoid letting children do so.

Massage

The simplest thing that you can do as a way of trying to make your pet feel more comfortable is to give it a regular massage, having checked with your vet beforehand that it will not cause any issues for your pet. Massaging your dog will help to build a bond of trust between you in the first instance, and can help to relieve your pet's pain, often bringing the added benefit of making you feel more relaxed as well. It can help to improve the circulation of both blood and lymph through the body.

If you are really wanting to help your pet in this way, then it will be well worth investing in training, with several different massage courses now available. If there is no course within easy reach of where you live, there is still the option of purchasing an informative DVD or taking online courses offered by practitioners working in this field, so that you can gain an understanding of what is involved in doing this safely and effectively. This may even open a new career for you, if you decide that you want to progress to gain a recognized qualification in this field, so that you can then treat other people's dogs in this way too.

Massage should be targeted to an individual dog's particular issues.

◄ *Massage can be beneficial in various ways. It will relax the muscles and improves circulation.*

Even in cases where joints are painful, this technique can help to lessen the pain by focusing on the associated supporting areas of muscle which provide support. It can also assist in reducing the stiffness or lameness that can follow a walk and help your dog to move more freely.

Alternatively, you can book regular massage sessions for your dog with a qualified practitioner, who will be able to devise the best routine for your pet. Remember that particularly athletic breeds that would normally run fast or over long distances can become excited when they are first let off the leash and are particularly vulnerable to muscular injuries as a result. They are unlikely to be in the peak of condition when they are first rehoused with you.

▼ *A range of different manual techniques can help your dog recover from injury and assist in relieving chronic pain.*

▼ *The massage technique will depend on the part of the body that is affected. Here, the abdomen is being massaged.*

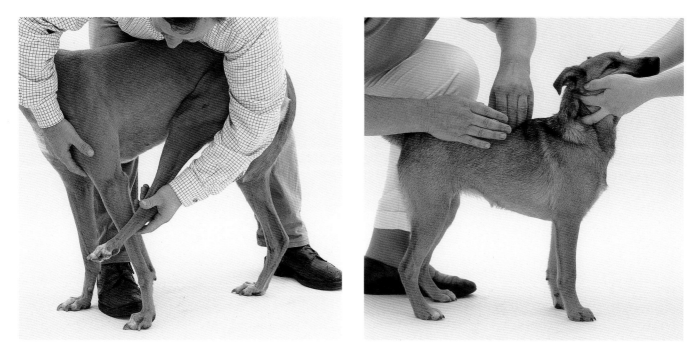

▲ *In this osteopathic examination, the hip is being flexed and articulated, with the hamstring muscles being stretched.*

▲ *A dog undergoing chiropractic treatment, with its spine being checked. This is another manipulative technique.*

It will help to undertake a preparatory warm up massage (especially when the weather is cold) and to massage your dog afterwards, to ease any aches or pains. By carefully managing your dog, and upping its exercise levels gradually, the risk of any injuries can be avoided, especially if you encourage your pet to run around in your garden at home.

Osteopathy

Whereas massage concentrates on the muscles that move the bones, osteopathy focuses on manipulating the underlying skeletal system. This technique developed from the theory that if there was a problem with the way that the skeleton was aligned, then the body itself would not be functioning correctly. Just as practised with human beings, osteopathy in dogs represents a combination of massage and joint manipulation.

Although recognized as being potentially beneficial under certain circumstances for dogs, there is no specific veterinary osteopathy training on offer. Your vet will therefore need to refer your dog to a human osteopath who also treats canine patients, and the osteopath will be obliged to follow the treatment recommended by the vet.

Not all dogs are suitable patients for osteopathy, especially those that are nervous, as they may actively resent being handled by a stranger while in pain. There are, however, a range of passive as well as active movements that an osteopath may use, and, combined with the massage element of this therapy, the results can be good, as reflected by greater mobility and less pain for your pet.

Chiropractic

This treatment is similar in some respects to osteopathy, and focuses on the vertebral column, linking to the nerves that connect to the spinal column here. Once again, this is a highly skilled treatment, and is never

something that you should attempt yourself.

There are only a relatively small number of trained veterinary chiropractors, but again, it is possible for your vet to refer you to a human chiropractor, if there is a possibility that this treatment could be beneficial. The theory is that if a bone within the spinal column is out of alignment with its neighbour, this will place pressure on the spinal cord and the nerves here, interfering with the nerve impulses and therefore the proper functioning of the limbs and organs.

Determining where in the spinal column that such misalignments may be present is key, before the necessary manipulation can be carried out to restore the correct positioning, which in turn will allow healing to take place. X-ray examinations are often a feature of chiropractic, allowing areas of abnormality to be seen and assessed.

Acupuncture for pain relief

The area of non-medicinal pain relief that has gained the most widespread acceptance in veterinary circles over recent years is acupuncture. This traditional form of Chinese medicine dates back thousands of years and has become much more widely used in veterinary care, to the extent that it should not be too difficult to track down a trained veterinary practitioner near you.

Acupuncture has been utilized for treating several conditions, particularly musculoskeletal problems causing pain, such as arthritis, hip dysplasia and spinal issues, although it can be used for conditions affecting other body systems too, notably of the intestinal tract, the skin and nervous system. Many veterinary health care policies now include cover to pay for acupuncture treatment. One area where acupuncture is contra-indicated, however, is in treating dogs that have cancers, because it may exacerbate the condition.

As this type of treatment has become more accepted in Western veterinary medicine, so the way it is used has become modified slightly from the original Chinese form, with the special acupuncture needles being inserted in set parts of the body for particular conditions. Interestingly, dogs generally do not resent having the acupuncture needles inserted into their bodies in any way, nor do they seek to remove them. In fact, in most cases, they appear to find the experience relaxing, and they have even been known to fall asleep during the treatment, revealing that it can be very calming for them. Acupuncture is particularly useful for chronic pain conditions, helping to relieve the pain without the need for painkillers.

Acupressure

Although you will not be able to carry out this treatment yourself, as it must be administered by a vet, what you can do to assist your dog more

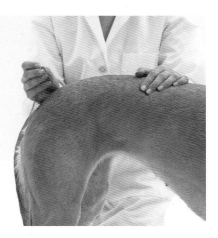

▲ *The most appropriate acupuncture points are selected based on various factors, including a clinical examination and the dog's history.*

directly, if it suffers from chronic pain, is to learn how to give acupressure. It is believed to be effective through causing the muscles to relax rather than remaining tense, which can exacerbate the pain. The same points are used as in acupuncture, but instead of needles, you use the tips of your fingers or even your fingernails for this purpose to apply pressure. Variations on this theme include more active massaging of the muscles, but you do need to be sure that you understand what you are doing, so as not to cause your pet pain as a result.

The theory

Both acupuncture and acupressure work based on Q'i (pronounced 'chee'), which describes the flow of energy through specific routes, with these

▼ *It is remarkable how well most dogs accept having acupuncture needles inserted into their bodies by a skilled practitioner.*

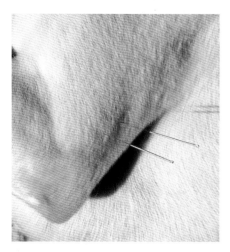

channels being known as meridians, although they are not a physical part of the body, like the nervous system for example. There are two opposite aspects in the body, as elsewhere in the universe, according to traditional Chinese medicine, in the form of 'yin' and 'yang'.

These complementary components occur together through the body, but yang predominates in the hollow organs, like the intestines or bladder whereas yin is present to a much greater extent in solid organs like the liver and kidneys. Paired meridians occur in conjunction with each organ, but in the body, there are two meridians that do not have pairs – these are the Governing Vessel and the Conception Vessel, which extend up the front of the body and down the back.

Acupuncture views the universe as being made of five different basic elements – fire, metal, earth, wood and water. These can inter-relate to each other, either positively or negatively. This means that while wood can give rise to fire, it will destroy earth.

According to acupuncture theory, diseases result from six environmental factors. These are summer heat, cold, the wind, dampness, dryness and heat. There are also eight conditions

◄ A growing number of veterinary practices offer acupuncture for dogs, and a major advantage is that it can offer pain relief in chronic cases without the need to resort to giving chemical painkillers regularly.

arising from four pairs of opposites, which are yin and yang, heat and cold, internal and external, plus excess and deficiency. All diseases are due to a combination of these eight conditions.

It is understanding and appreciating the relationships between these eight conditions of opposites, the five elements, and the six environmental factors that is central to acupuncture theory. This knowledge serves to indicate which points on a particular meridian can be used to bring Q'i back into balance, thereby proving how, with harmony in the body restored, the natural healing forces can effect a cure.

▼ A dog undergoing acupuncture treatment combined with moxibustion, using a burning herbal stick of dried mugwort.

HOW ACUPUNCTURE DEVELOPED

There is no actual medicine prescribed with acupuncture, although on occasions, a special burning herbal stick made up of dried mugwort may be used as part of the treatment to stimulate the acupuncture point. This is known as moxibustion. The key is to determine the precise points along the meridian where the stimulation needs to be applied to achieve this goal, with the underlying knowledge having been built up over thousands of years.

In the early days, a form of acupressure was used, after which sharp fragments of bamboo and sometimes bone were utilized, being inserted into the body at the appropriate points. Nowadays, special fine steel surgical needles are utilized for acupuncture treatment.

Natural treatments to aid recovery

Perhaps the best-known method of treatment to aid recovery from an injury is physiotherapy. It is a versatile option, that will both aid the healing process and reduce pain, and can be used in conjunction with other treatments. The heated water of a hydrotherapy pool has many advantages in aiding recovery and the gentle healing powers of Reiki can also help in this process.

Physiotherapy

Veterinary physiotherapists who are used to having animals as patients are to be recommended, partly because they will have undergone additional training in anatomy, having first qualified as human physiotherapists. In addition, they will be used to dealing with dogs that are likely to be in pain and will need careful handling. Once again, however, you will need a veterinary referral.

The aim is to ensure your dog regains its strength and a full range of movement in its joints. Aside from direct manipulation of the affected area, physiotherapy may also involve a variety of other techniques, including the use of electrical stimulation of the affected area, to build muscle strength and improve the circulation.

Lasers are also now being used in the canine physiotherapy field, as a means of aiding blood flow and releasing muscle tension that can be caused by pain. The use of electrical stimulation to trigger contraction of the muscles, and counter muscle wasting, is commonly utilized in physiotherapy, and can also improve the circulation.

Heat and cold can be used within the field of physiotherapy as well. Ultrasound, which provides warmth by means of the ultrasonic vibrations, is particularly useful in restricting the amount of scar tissue that forms after injury and may otherwise restrict the dog's range of movements. This can be combined with stretching exercises, to increase the degree of flexibility, with each patient having a separate recovery plan matched to their individual requirements.

Hydrotherapy

Alongside physiotherapy, hydrotherapy may often be recommended by vets as part of an exercise recovery programme. This form of therapy extends back to the early days of greyhound racing in the 19th century. Today, there are canine hydrotherapy pools in most major cities, and it offers a form of low-impact exercise, as the buoyancy of the water helps to support your pet's weight.

Hydrotherapy is very useful for an older dog suffering with painful joints. The temperature-controlled warmth of the water, which is heated to approximately 30°C (86°F), also serves to decrease swelling. The heated water helps by improving the dog's circulation, in a way that is not offered by swimming in cooler surroundings.

The dog is eased into the water gently, down a special ramp, or by means of a hoist, and wears a special buoyancy jacket with a harness attached. A trained therapist will go into the pool with your dog, determining the length of the session. Some breeds of dog are more instinctively drawn to water than others, but interestingly, virtually all dogs take to hydrotherapy well, and show the benefits, although at first, they may need a bit of coaxing to enter the water.

◄ *The recovery period for older dogs suffering from injuries is likely to be more protracted than in the case of younger individuals.*

► *Assisting a dog's recovery from injury requires a thorough understanding of canine anatomy.*

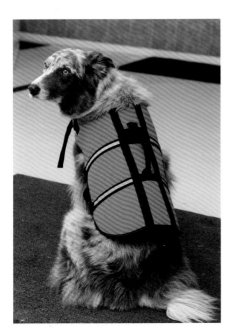

▲ *Wearing a suitable flotation jacket will give a nervous or handicapped dog some confidence before it enters the water.*

▲ *The dog is constantly supervised while undergoing hydrotherapy, and it can bring noticeable benefits, especially for older dogs.*

In certain cases, rather than using a relatively large pool, a water treadmill is recommended. It is rather like a narrow corridor, with glass sides, and the floor area consists of a moving treadmill. The water level in the unit is raised to the appropriate level, to support the dog, and it is possible to watch how the dog is moving through the glass panels at the side.

You need to prepare your dog for hydrotherapy, by grooming it first, so there will no loose hair when it enters the pool. Withhold food for several hours beforehand, partly because this should help to ensure that your pet does not relieve itself in the water, always encouraging it to do so beforehand if possible.

Reiki

There are some other options in terms of therapy that may sometimes be used, notably Reiki. Reputedly first used by Buddha about 2,500 years

ago, knowledge of this practice had largely become lost, until rediscovered and subsequently promoted by a Japanese doctor called Dr Mikao Usui during the late 1800s.

The energy from Reiki, as reflected by 'Rei' in its name, is universal. 'Ki' describes the life force that serves as the healing energy. As a result, this

means that this energy can be used for any animal, including dogs, just as much as for people.

Once again, you still need to consult a vet if your dog is in pain, but Reiki may aid its recovery as an adjunct to other treatment. This practice is also valued as a way of keeping your dog fit and well.

▼ *A Reiki practitioner at work. The hands are positioned to channel healing energies, rather than to manipulate the joints directly.*

Natural ways to calm a nervous dog

Many rescue dogs can prove to be nervous by nature, especially in the early days after moving to a new home. While reassurance will help, and the situation will improve over time as you build a bond and routine with your new pet, there are various natural treatments and techniques that you can utilize, in the hope that they will aid your dog in settling down.

Bach flower remedies

Perhaps not surprisingly, plants and flowers have a long history of use as a source of compounds that can be used for therapeutic purposes. The energy of plants was utilized by the pioneering homeopathic doctor, Dr Samuel Hahnemann. Subsequently, in the 20th century, Dr Edward Bach, who had studied homeopathy, felt that disease developed in the mind, and set out to find plants that could be utilized by way of treatment, coming up with his own set of remedies, that still bear his name.

The way in which the tincture is prepared was very important, and this included the time of day and the weather conditions, according to Dr Bach. As an example, if it became cloudy during this process, in the case of spring and summer-flowering plants, the batch created using the

▲ Herbal remedies may be helpful in helping to overcome a dog's fear, with white chestnut offering tranquillity.

fresh flowers in spring water was discarded. Purity was vital, in Dr Bach's view, and the flowers had to be gathered from unpolluted areas in the wild and prepared using spring water. Those gathered in winter were processed by boiling them. In each case, the resulting energized water was then mixed with brandy in the human version (making them unsuitable for dogs) and the resulting solution is then significantly diluted before being used.

Bach proposed that the natural vibrations of particular plants in the tinctures can reset the incorrect vibrations that arise with certain mental states. Interestingly, although clinical tests have struggled to

highlight how and why Bach flower remedies work, the testimony of many dog owners is that they can have a positive impact on their pets.

These remedies can be acquired individually, with heather often being advocated for separation anxiety for example, but generally, the combined form, featuring five separate remedies and known as Rescue Remedy, is the most widely used form today, as far as dogs are concerned.

Owners tend to turn to Rescue Remedy for a nervous dog, especially one that is badly affected by noise, such as from fireworks or a thunderstorm. It can also be used to help a nervous dog travel in a vehicle, with the aim of preventing it from becoming distressed. Nevertheless, aim to address the underlying issues, rather than relying on Rescue Remedy on a long-term basis, especially for car travel.

▼ Since only drops are required, it is usually very easy to administer Bach flower remedies to your dog.

▲ Homeopathic remedies are devised on a different basis to conventional medications, with just trace amounts of the key ingredient being present.

▲ If you can persuade your dog to open its mouth readily, you may be able to dose it directly – or at least conceal the tablet in food.

▲ Liquid drops can also be disguised using food, provided they are not particularly strong-smelling, which could be off-putting.

Homeopathy

Although also rather controversial, in terms of how it may be of benefit, homeopathy nevertheless has a long tradition, extending back some 300 years. A key practical difference is that unlike Bach flower remedies, certain homeopathic remedies come in tablet form. This can make administering them to a dog more difficult, especially if it is rather nervous, and will not allow you to open its mouth.

Homeopathy operates based on 'like cures like', and its founder, Dr

▼ It is a good idea to train dogs to take medication directly, as there will be times when this is necessary.

Samuel Hahnemann, observed how taking a non-lethal quantity of a poison could result in healing a disease that was similar in its impact on the body to that of the poison. Treatment depends on the dilution of the solution, with vigorous shaking, called potentizing, being vital.

The way in which homeopathy remedies are described is in terms of their potency. This in turn refers to the number of dilutions that they have undergone, based on Latin numerals, so that a figure of 'X' or 'D' refers to 10, 'C' is 100 and 'LM' is 50,000. As a general guide, a 30C potency is used for emergency situations, with aconite often being recommended for emotional stress and panic attacks in dogs.

Tissue salts are also used as a branch of homeopathy. These remedies were derived on the basis that there were 12 salts in the body that could be used to treat mild cases and correct deficiencies of mineral salts, with Kali. phos. being the remedy of choice to address emotional stress. There are homeopathic vets who can prescribe the most appropriate remedy for your pet.

CBD SUPPLEMENTS

With the legalization of cannabis-growing recently, notably in parts of the USA, various CBD (or cannabidiol) products derived from marijuana plants are now finding their way into the pet market, both as a way of providing pain relief and as a way of addressing anxiety issues. However, at this stage, there is currently little evidence to show that they are beneficial, especially when it comes to treating anxiety, although greatest promise may lie in the field of epilepsy treatments.

CBD products lack the active tetrahydrocannabinol (THC) component of cannabis which is well-known for its psychoactive effects. Under no circumstances should dogs ever be administered with marijuana or indeed, a THC product, as these can have seriously harmful and long-lasting effects on them.

CHAPTER FIVE

TROUBLESHOOTING

It is hard to appreciate the amount of trauma and physical suffering that some dogs experience before they pass into the care of a rescue. It is therefore not surprising that they often have behavioural issues as a consequence. Behavioural problems may have arisen based upon their past experiences. For example, if they have been left alone for long periods, they may soil in the home or destroy things, and then they could have suffered physical abuse as a 'punishment' for their behaviour. While many behavioural issues can be addressed successfully by training, it can be much harder to address problems linked to physical abuse, where there has been a loss of trust in people. In this instance particularly, you will need to be patient, with time serving as a significant healer. You must allow your dog to build up trust in you and other family members.

Much of this can be done by adopting a positive attitude on your part, establishing a strong bond with your pet over time. The tone of voice is a powerful way of communicating, and even if your pet behaves in a way that is not desirable, avoid shouting or even worse, hitting your pet. This is likely to be incredibly damaging. Always remain calm and adopt a stern tone that your dog will realise indicates all is not well.

Try to encourage your dog to behave as you want, by guidance. It will instinctively seek to gain your approval and praising your pet is very important when it behaves as you want. This so-called 'positive reinforcement' helps to emphasize the learning message that you are seeking to convey to your pet.

◄ *Just as you will need to learn about your dog and its habits, so it too will need to learn about you and its new home. Things will not always go smoothly, and you will need to be patient on occasions.*

Issues around food

Dogs by nature are keen to eat, although this may not always be the food that you provide! Most will instinctively take food if it is within reach, even if this not intended for them, especially if there is no-one around. On the other hand, there can sometimes be situations where a dog displays little or no interest in its food. Dogs can also become possessive about their food, which will need addressing.

An unexplained loss of appetite tends to be a problem more commonly seen in small dogs, and may reflect illness, or possibly a dental issue. It can also be linked with the type of food, as most dogs prefer wet food over dry food, and changing this can impact positively on the appetite of a reluctant feeder.

Seeking attention

With small dogs, and particularly those of Chihuahua lineage, loss of appetite can sometimes be linked with apparent attention-seeking, developing over time. The dog starts to refuse its food but will take it from you when being offered food by hand, and then wants to be fed in this way going forwards.

Small dogs are very good at manipulating their owners, learning fast how to do so, rather like a child

▼ Dental issues are often a reason as to why dogs find it difficult (and painful) to eat dry food in particular.

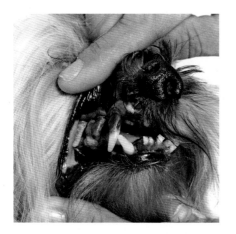

▲ A raised feeding bowl is useful for dogs at risk of bloat or suffering from neck pain which makes it uncomfortable to eat at ground level.

feigning illness to avoid school, so beware! Missing an odd meal should not be an issue, but if you allow this habit to develop, it can soon become a problem. Have your pet checked out by your vet, to ensure there is nothing physically wrong, and then change the feeding routine and probably the food on offer.

Possible solutions

It may be a good idea to invest in a bigger feeding bowl, with lower sides, or even try an old saucer, in case your dog feels that it is rather boxed-in with a small food container. You could alternatively try a raised feeder, which is recommended for dogs with neck pain, as they do not have to bend to eat. Switch where in the home you are feeding your dog, and it may be worth trying either to mix in a different food or adding just

a few palatable treats to what you are currently offering.

Another thing to try may be to offer lesser amounts of food and increase the number of meals that you provide through the day. Large dogs may only be fed once, but small dogs should have their food ration divided into two portions, and this can be expanded to four under these circumstances. The idea is that hopefully your dog will be hungry and keener to eat as a result.

The other thing to ensure is that other members of the family are not offering more tempting titbits under the table, so your dog is obtaining food elsewhere.

▲ *Dogs often become excited when offered food, but never tease your dog by taking away its meal if it refuses to sit.*

▲ *It will take time to teach your pet, but your dog will learn that if it sits, then it will be able to eat more quickly.*

Possessiveness over food

This issue is relatively common and can lead to serious displays of aggression if the situation escalates. It is particularly important therefore never to feed two dogs in the same space at the same time, because one individual may gulp down its food faster than the other and may attempt to steal its companion's meal. This in turn can lead to an aggressive response, initially in terms of body language and then actual conflict, if the first dog does not back down.

Nor is it just with another dog that this issue may arise. While a dog can often get excitable when it is about to be fed, some individuals are very reluctant to let you take their bowl away, even once they have finished their food. Under these circumstances, the dog will sit or lie by the bowl, and starts growling if you try to pick up the empty container, even snapping at you, should you try to remove it.

▶ *Food possessiveness is a serious issue. The dog will growl menacingly and will strike out if you attempt to take the bowl away. Throwing a treat into the bowl may help to break down this aggression as your dog realises it can gain a reward from your presence.*

Hopefully, you will be aware of this issue, based on the experiences of the rescue centre. The cause is often that in its past life, the dog was teased with food, having had it offered and taken away, and now feels inclined to assert itself. In the most extreme cases, a dog may even bite.

What you do not want, if your dog is simply displaying mild signs of possessiveness over food, is for the situation to escalate further. In the first place, if the dog is known to have had a troubled past, it is very important to feed your pet at consistent times. This will help to give it reassurance.

It is also vital to try and ascertain exactly what the issue revolves around, in terms of your dog's behaviour. Some individuals act like this because they are trying to assert their dominance, whereas others are nervous. It will help to establish some rules before putting the food bowl on the floor. Do not allow your dog to jump around but encourage it to sit. Then produce the food bowl at this point. Never offer the food bowl and then take it away, before letting your pet eat its food, because this is likely to exacerbate the situation.

Another thing that you can try is to distract your dog away from its bowl after it has eaten, with a favourite toy. You do not want to get into a full-on game or encourage your pet to run at this stage though, because of the risk of bloat and torsion developing, which is a particular risk with narrow-chested breeds, but simply call it out of the room where it has been fed, using the toy as necessary.

Problems surrounding food can usually be overcome once your dog realizes that it will be fed regularly, and it does not have to battle for a

◄ *Hand-feeding can be useful in various situations, such as if your dog is reluctant to feed. Offer food in the palm of your hand to avoid the risk of an accidental nip to your fingers.*

meal, as it may have done if it was living on the streets with other dogs previously. You should notice an improvement over time, which will be detectable based on your dog's body language.

Addressing possessiveness

It is always a good idea to exercise your dog before feeding it, should it display signs of food possessiveness. After you get back, it is likely to be more tired, and will simply want to eat and then curl up and sleep, rather than remaining in the vicinity of the food bowl, particularly if you call it to you and reward it with a treat elsewhere in the home. This will act as a distraction, drawing the dog away from its bowl once it is empty.

You can also vary how you provide your pet's food. Put on a disposable vinyl glove and pick up some of its food. Then offer this where you would normally feed your dog, calling it to you, and ensuring the food is in the palm of your hand, tilting this downwards while keeping your fingers and thumb together. Your dog should then soon eat the food, taking it off your outstretched hand, although you need to hold your hand in such a way that there is

no danger of getting your fingers bitten.

Once this is working well, you can then reintroduce a feeding bowl, but vary things so your dog will be uncertain as to how it will be fed. You will soon recognize when things are improving, because the dog's body language will be more relaxed in the vicinity of the food bowl.

It will not be so inclined to stay near the bowl once it has finished eating but will amble off once it realizes there is no more food there.

Curing this possessiveness can be a protracted issue in some cases and may require a flexible approach. As with all behavioural problems, you need to be patient and encourage your pet, as you work together to achieve the desired outcome.

Preventing thieving

Stealing food is a serious issue with dogs, although some individuals are more inclined to behave in this way than others. Scenthounds such as Beagles, which evolved to live in packs, tend to be worse in this respect than some other types of dogs.

Most dogs will not steal from directly in front of you, but if you leave a bag of shopping on the floor and wander off, the chances are that it will be investigated by your pet, and any particularly tasty items such as meat will be pulled out and carried off to be consumed elsewhere.

The situation can be worse with tall dogs capable of taking food directly off a kitchen work surface for example. This is where there will be more food potentially within easy reach, with such individuals using their height effectively, being able to stand up on their hind legs. Even so, smaller individuals will adapt and use their ingenuity to reach items when this is possible. Do not leave chairs

◄ *Thieving is something that many dogs will do instinctively, if the opportunity presents itself, particularly if they have been forced to scavenge in the past. Always aim to anticipate the risk, by not leaving food unattended and within reach.*

▶ *Dogs are quite willing to steal from kitchen bins, and uncooked raw meat or out-of-date food could result in serious digestive upsets. A more secure container for kitchen waste will be required.*

out in front of a table where there is food for example, as you may well find that your dog jumps up on to the chair and then on to the table.

Should this happen, it is very frustrating but is basically a reflection of your dog's natural opportunistic instinct to take advantage of available food. The simplest solution is to prevent the situation arising in the first place. If you haven't had a dog before, your mindset may need to change somewhat, in terms of not leaving tempting items of food accessible within the home.

Showing initiative!

Dogs can be very resourceful when it comes to food, even to the point of learning how to open the door to a refrigerator, so that it can be advisable to fit a child-proof lock here if necessary. Potentially more harmful to your pet, however, will be the opportunity to raid the rubbish bin, where there could be bones and the remains of raw meat items, which are likely to represent a serious health risk. Even a small dog is able to reach its contents, by knocking the bin over, so you may need to invest in a new rubbish container.

When you are eating, it is not necessarily a good idea to allow your dog into the room with you, especially if you have young children. Otherwise, you may find that they start to slip food from their plates to the dog. This can very quickly develop into a habit as far as your

pet is concerned, and it will look to be fed with titbits in this way on a regular basis. This can quite easily result in your dog putting on weight over time, and it can end up with your dog trying to grab food from the hand as well, in the mistaken belief that a treat is being provided.

Abnormal appetite

Described as pica, one of the most common displays of this behaviour can be when you are out walking, and your dog decides to eat cow pats or horse dung, perhaps. The reasons underlying this unpleasant behaviour are not clear. It has been suggested that there may be B vitamins and possibly beneficial bacteria present in the dung of herbivores, but equally, if you have a cat, you may find that your dog is drawn to its litter tray as well.

Dealing with this situation depends on the surroundings in part, as obviously, you need to empty a soiled cat litter tray without delay in any case, and your dog must be on a leash in the vicinity of any farm stock like cattle or sheep. Overall, though, you will need to work on the general training of your dog so that it will learn to come back to you without hesitation, when called, and understands the meaning of the phrase 'drop', which is most easily taught through play.

One particularly unpleasant trait that may be evident in dogs that have spent much of their lives in

kennels is that they will eat their faeces, within the confines of the garden. The reason may be linked to a desire to keep their surroundings clean, although it has also been suggested that this behaviour may indicate a shortage of B vitamins, which are not stored in the body. It may be worthwhile getting a supplement which can be added to your pet's food if it is on a wet diet.

The other thing to do is to remove temptation at once, essentially by calling your dog indoors immediately after it has relieved itself, allowing you to clear up the mess straight away. This will hopefully break the habit, which is less likely to be displayed when you are out on a walk, although here, clearing up after your pet is usually a legal obligation.

▼ *Unfortunately, dogs often find cowpats and herbivore dung in general appealing to eat, especially when it is dry.*

Problems around handling your dog

Dogs which have not been used to being handled by people or have been subject to physical abuse in the past are likely to resent being restrained for handling purposes. It will be important to work on this issue though, because there are a surprising number of occasions when you will need to handle your pet, for example when grooming, checking the coat for ticks and fleas, or cleaning their teeth.

If you can't hold your rescue dog closely without the risk of being bitten and must resort to muzzling your pet on every occasion it will become very stressful for both of you. Proceed carefully when you first acquire your dog, because although this may not have been an issue at the rescue centre, it could well be a problem until you have established a bond of trust with your pet. Also, you may find that it is simply certain things, such as picking up your dog's paw or stroking their head that

▼ Not all dogs may have become familiarized with being picked up in puppyhood, so reassurance will be required.

upsets your pet, rather than being groomed, for example.

Especially in the early days, always stroke your dog gently, reassuring it so that it learns that there is no reason to become upset. When you start to do something new, proceed cautiously and always watch your dog's reaction, to give you an insight into what it will tolerate.

If you notice that it starts to become upset, based on its body language, you may need to rethink what you are doing. Its stance will change, resulting in its posture becoming more rigid. Then if its distress increases further, it will start growling and may snap at you.

▲ The key thing when carrying a dog is that it feels secure, so that it will not struggle and end up scratching you.

Picking your dog up

It is much easier picking up a small dog rather than a large individual, but the same technique applies. You want to encircle your dog's body if possible, supporting your pet as you lift it up, so that it feels secure and will not struggle.

This will mean either wrapping your arms horizontally around your dog's body, and lifting it up, or doing so by placing your hand under its chest, between its front legs. With small dogs, you can effectively do this by placing your arm around its chest, tucking its hindquarters into the crook of your arm as you do so, and being sure to direct your pet's face away from yours at this stage.

Do not be surprised if your dog attempts to struggle at first. Hopefully, once it realizes that it is

▲ *Many dogs can be nervous about having their feet touched, let alone having their nails clipped as shown here.*

▲ *Being able to pick up your dog safely and securely is very important, particularly as it becomes older.*

secure, and is not going to fall, then it will cease behaving in this way. But ensure that its head is directed away from your face, and bear in mind that you could get scratched. You may want to put your hand on its collar, to give a bit more control. It is not a good idea to combine two novel experiences, in terms of being picked up and put in a bath for example, as part of the same process – get your dog used to being picked up as the starting point.

Paws and claws

A common reason why dogs dislike having their paws touched is claw-clipping. If your dog has had its claws cut too short previously, this will have been a painful experience, and the chances are that it could have remembered having its paws held for this purpose. It is much better to leave this task to your vet, when required.

The paws are a very sensitive area of a dog's body, and even in cases where your dog normally does not resent having its feet held up, you will need to be very careful if you

spot that your pet is licking one of its paws repeatedly. If you try to inspect this in a casual way at this stage, the chances are that you could easily end up being bitten. There may be a grass seed here, acting like a splinter, or even mites causing irritation. Irrespective of the cause, the pain is likely to make your dog react badly under these circumstances.

When you start to lift your dog's paws, do so when your dog is relaxed, and sitting with you. Start by stroking the paws and then gently lift a front paw with your hand. This will give you a clear indication of whether your dog is happy for you to do so. Avoid doing this for the first time when you are grooming your pet, because you may encounter more of a reaction if your dog is unhappy.

Ear issues

Some dogs also dislike having their ears touched. In the case of spaniel-type breeds, with their long, heavy ears overlapping over the ear canals, this can be indicative of a painful infection. There is often a rather unpleasant odour present, and you will need to get your pet checked out by your vet, obtaining appropriate treatment as necessary.

In other instances, it may possibly be that your dog has had its ears twisted in the past, which will obviously have been painful, and/or it is simply wary of having your hands approaching its head. You will need to win your pet's confidence, as it is important to be able to inspect your pet's ears on a regular basis. Start by stroking the head, and work your hand down over the ears, gently starting to raise them. Before long, this should not be a problem, but take particular care if the hair here is knotted, as grooming will then be painful for your pet.

▼ *Being able to look in your dog's ear is important. Train it to accept you doing so while you are making a fuss of your pet.*

Control issues

Many dogs are enthusiastic about the sight of a leash, associating it with going for a walk, but this enthusisasm needs to be controlled. For a minority, however, a leash can represent memories of a disturbed past, and solving this issue will require a different approach. You also need to be alert to what your dog puts into its mouth when out walking in case it is in danger of harming itself.

A dog's collar serves several purposes: carrying its identity medallion, providing a means of attaching its leash, and to assist in controlling it at close quarters, if, for example, it appears to be wanting to run off. However, not all dogs like having their collars restrained. This can be a particular problem when you want to take your dog for a walk, if it regularly starts to jump around excitedly so that you cannot attach the leash. What you need to do is to train your dog to 'sit', and then remain in this position while you attach the leash to its collar. Obviously, this is a routine that you can practise independently, but equally, it is something that you can concentrate on should you take your dog to training classes.

It is important to work on this issue at home, because once you start going out with your dog, and letting it off the leash, you need to have the certainty that not only will your pet return readily to you when called, but also, that you will be able to put it back on its leash without difficulty when necessary.

Start by calling your dog to you in the garden and praise it when it comes to you. If you know your dog is headstrong and reluctant to be put back on its leash, do not make an immediate attempt to grab at its collar. It will otherwise start to see this as a game. Exercising a dog with a harness can be easier, as getting hold of this is more straightforward than trying to catch an individual using its collar.

What you want to happen is for your dog to come to you when called, and then sit still, rather than jumping around, so you can put the leash on without difficulty. One of the reasons that it is important to practise this routine at home is because otherwise, your dog will become excited, on the basis that the only time that it sees its leash is when it is being taken out for a walk. This will make it harder to control. (For more advice on training your dog to 'sit', see page 164.)

Bad experiences in the past

Aside from running around and jumping up excitedly, another issue that can occur with putting your dog on a leash is that it may suddenly roll over onto its back and wriggle

▲ *When you are out with your dog, do not let your pet lose focus. Call it back to you and praise it when it responds accordingly.*

◄ *It is much easier to train your dog at home, where there are far fewer distractions in terms of interesting scents.*

◄ You need to be particularly focused in urban areas, such as parks, where there will be more dogs around. Be sure your dog is well-socialized before letting it free.

► There may be busy roads bordering a park. You need to be in full control of your pet at all times.

around on the ground. This is typically a sign of submissive behaviour and tends to be more common in bitches. Some individuals will even urinate while lying in this position on their back, with this behaviour being especially common in the case of dogs that have been badly mistreated in the past.

It may be that your pet had been hit regularly at some point in the past with its leash, and this memory has made it fearful when it sees a leash. If you suspect that this is the case, it

▼ Certain types of dogs, particularly those with a scenthound ancestry, can be harder to persuade to return to you.

is possible that your pet may respond more favourably to a harness, or alternatively, try an extendable leash.

As time passes, so you will soon come to recognize how your dog behaves, and hopefully, will notice an improvement. If, when handling your pet, it unexpectedly becomes aggressive when you pick it up, this is then highly indicative of an underlying health problem rather than a behavioural issue and is likely to require veterinary advice.

An emergency situation

There may be occasions when your dog has picked up something that could be dangerous to its health, which you need to retrieve urgently, without having to risk opening its mouth, in case your pet swallows something that could be potentially fatal. This is a situation where you need to raid your fridge, and offer something that your dog will find irresistible, such as a piece of meat or cheese, or call your dog to you for a treat if you are out. Always make sure that you have something of this type when you are out together.

In an emergency, drop a couple of pieces of the tasty snack on the floor near your pet or even throw them to

get its attention if you are not very close. It will then hopefully need to let go of the dangerous item, to pick up the food. Rather than making an immediate dash for it, persuade your pet to walk further away, aiming to place yourself between the item and your pet, throwing more food treats to increase the distance between them. This will then make it easier either to pick up the item, without your dog becoming possessive and rushing back to it or having to put your pet immediately on the leash.

▼ There are various household items that could make your dog seriously unwell, or even prove fatal – including chocolate.

Garden play concerns

Dogs by nature are playful, and this activity provides an excellent way to bond with your pet. Even in the case of street dogs which have never had the opportunity to play, they will soon learn to do so. Play also helps their co-ordination and fitness, with gentle play being of real benefit right through into old age. There can be occasions, however, when things go wrong, and problems must be addressed.

◄ *A young dog indicates its readiness to play, engaging in a so-called 'play bow' by extending and lowering its front legs.*

It will not take long for your dog to appreciate that if it wants to play, then it will need to bring the toy back to you and drop it, which will be a valuable lesson learnt, and once that comes quite naturally both you and your dog will be able to relax.

The more powerful dogs, even medium-sized dogs like those which have Staffordshire bull terrier in their ancestry, often like to engage in tests of strength, using a tug toy. You hold one side, and the dog pulls on the other. This may be accompanied by quite a bit of noise on your pet's part, but this is typically good-natured. Nevertheless, you do not want a game of tug to get out of hand, nor do you want your pet to injure itself, so do not let this situation arise! If you feel this could

The type of toy that you choose for your dog will impact on its behaviour, and the way that it behaves in play sessions. Almost all dogs like chasing after a ball of suitable size, which they can pick up in their mouths, but cannot inadvertently swallow or puncture. In its enthusiasm though, your dog may fail to realize that it should return with the ball to you once it has caught it. The same is true of other toys, like flying discs.

This is especially likely if your pet is not used to this type of game. What you need to do is to call your dog back to you, once it has the toy in its mouth, and encourage it to drop the toy. Depending partly on how

confident you are, you can gently open the dog's mouth, remove the toy, and throw it again, or you can simply walk away and express no more interest in the game. Do not scold your dog if it fails to let go of the toy initially.

► *If left unsupervised, some dogs like to dig and will bury items in the ground, with a view to retrieving them later.*

▶ *A toddler or young child should never be left to play with a dog unsupervised, as either could end up inadvertently hurting the other. Even a small dog can knock over a child by jumping up.*

be happening, then the best solution is to drop the toy and walk away. Your dog is likely to continue chewing on it for a few minutes but will soon lose interest.

Supervision required

Issues are most likely to arise in the case of younger dogs when it comes to play, because they prove to be more excitable at this stage in life anyway. They are also more inclined to test the limits of what is acceptable, especially if they have had no proper training. It is important to keep a tight grip on the situation, because otherwise, things can escalate out of control, and particularly if you have children, this can become potentially dangerous.

What can happen is that your pet becomes over-excitable, running around and jumping up trying to take the toy. Then when you do throw it, the dog runs off with it and may be reluctant to return when called, expecting you to chase off after it, which is what you need to avoid. Then as your pet tires, it may want to lie down with the toy, but growls at you if you try to take it away and could easily snap at you if you do not appreciate the hint.

Possessiveness

With all dog toys, possessiveness can be an issue in some situations. Dogs which have displayed this characteristic in other areas, with food for example, are likely to behave in a similar way

with toys. Do not be fooled either – some of the worst offenders in terms of possessive behaviour with regard to toys can be the smallest dogs, such as Chihuahuas, Pomchis (Pomeranian-Chihuahua crosses) and similar types of dogs.

The problem can be that what may start out as a seemingly minor issue, such as refusing to drop a toy, can escalate into a much more serious situation. This can happen with dogs that have not been

properly trained in the past, which is why it is always very important to work on your dog's basic training consistently from the outset. Teaching 'sit' is a crucial lesson not just for safety, when your dog could be entering a dangerous situation, but also because it provides a way to distract your pet from its possessive

▼ *Always aim to play well away from other dogs, which may want to move in on a game and steal your pet's toy.*

◄ One of the things older children should be taught is that they should not cause the dog to become overexcited when playing, causing it to jump up and bark.

behaviour. You then need to reinforce the lesson of 'drop', so your dog releases the toy onto the ground. When this happens, offer a reward some distance away and immediately afterwards, pick up the toy while your dog is eating its treat.

If you find that your dog tends to persist in behaving in this way, do not allow it to have constant access to that toy. Once you have taken the toy away, keep it until you start another game. Begin then by persuading your dog to sit, rather than rushing up and grabbing the toy, or chasing after it, just as in the same way, you ensure your dog sits before putting its food bowl on the floor. The message in both cases is the same: your dog has to understand that you are in charge.

You need to be sure that your dog learns to follow the same basic rules, whether you are offering food, putting it on a leash or playing a game. The most critical thing is that you are in control; there are situations where this could potentially

save your dog's life. 'Drop' and 'come' are other general instructions that your dog must master. In all these situations, clicker training can be very helpful, reinforcing the verbal instruction, so that ultimately, it will become second nature to your pet to behave in this way. (For further advice on clicker training and general training see pages 74–5 and 162–171).

There is no way of knowing whether your dog will be possessive with its toys. In fact, dogs are very individual in terms of their preferences. Some may be possessive over a ball,

► Dogs which have not been well-socialized can prove to be aggressive when meeting other dogs, irrespective of their size, and this will be revealed by their body language. It is something that you will need to work on with your pet.

but not with a chew toy, although often, it is toys in this latter category that are more likely to be guarded, because as they are chewable, they can be seen in the same category as food.

It also has to be said, however, that a few dogs express little or no interest in chasing a ball or playing with other types of toy even when they see companions behaving in this way. This is not a cause for any concern.

Bear in mind also that dogs are most likely to challenge a younger member of a family who tries to take a toy away, even with the intention of wanting to play a game with it. Therefore it is very important to address possessiveness seriously, discuss this with the rescue staff and seek professional training advice as necessary. It is one of the most common reasons that dogs are returned to rescues, and equally why rescues are very cautious about re-homing dogs into an environment where there are young children.

▶ *The cat's body language here is showing that it is not entirely relaxed, while the dog is watching carefully, and has a rather playful demeanour, with no sign of its hackles being raised.*

Boredom

It is never a good idea to leave your dog alone in your garden for any length of time, especially with a toy. You may find that your dog has started to dig in a flower bed, usually choosing an area where the soil is relatively soft, making it easier to bury the toy.

It is thought that this behaviour may be linked back to the way in which wild canids, such as the grey wolf, sought to hide surplus food by concealing it, where it will be less likely to be discovered by scavengers. Certain types of dogs, notably those with a terrier ancestry, such as the Staffordshire bull terrier, the Border terrier and the Jack Russell, are more likely to behave in this way than others, given that this behaviour was ingrained in their working past.

A bored dog often seeks to tunnel out under a fence and explore the wider world if left in the garden to play by itself. It is a good idea to identify any weak spots in your

perimeter fencing and check these regularly for any signs of digging. Placing large stones here or sinking slates into the ground adjacent to the fence line should help to frustrate your dog's attempts.

Unneutered male dogs are most likely to stray, notably if they pick up the scent of a bitch in heat nearby. Even though your dog may have been neutered, it will take time for the benefit of this surgery to become apparent, in terms of his behaviour, because of the hormones still present in the body. These will decline to the stage that six weeks or so after surgery, you will detect noticeable benefits, to the extent that his personality will be calmer and his interest in the opposite sex will also decline. Even so, it is worth bearing in mind that just because he has been castrated, he will still be able to mate with a bitch in these early stages and this could still give rise to unwanted puppies.

◀ *Dogs with broad, powerful mouths enjoy chew or tug toys, but they must be taught to let go of the item when they are told to do so.*

Potential conflict

Sometimes, dogs can get distracted when they are playing in the garden, often by cats – either yours or someone else's cat which comes into your garden. As mentioned earlier, cats that have grown up in the company of dogs usually adopt a much more robust approach, even stopping and staring down their canine chaser and hissing menacingly.

Many dogs usually get the message very quickly, but especially in the case of dogs with a high prey drive that have been bred to hunt, such as lurchers, the situation can be much trickier, and they will not be able to live with a cat. Again, this is something critical that rescue organizations aim to focus on when it comes to re-homing.

If there are neighbourhood cats that enter your garden, it will be a good idea to check before you let your dog out that none are present. Otherwise, just as when taking your dog out for a walk in the park or countryside, you will need to muzzle it so that it can cause no harm. Hound crosses of this type can accelerate very quickly, catching a cat unawares.

Separation anxiety

Anxieties about being separated are common, particularly if you leave your dog alone in the home for any length of time. It may have been left alone for long periods in the past and doesn't trust that you will return. Near neighbours may also be upset, as your dog may – unbeknown to you – start barking for long periods, which is a likely sign of separation anxiety.

Being social by nature, a dog will want to spend its time as part of the family, which it views rather as a pack. This is not all about being fussed over – dogs are often very content just to sleep by their owners during the day, even if there is no direct interaction between them. A dog that has built up a close bond with its new owner can suffer if the routine of daily life suddenly changes.

◄ A dog sits in a window barking, waiting for its owner to return. This is typical behaviour associated with separation anxiety. Speak with your vet about using a natural remedy like Zylkene® or Adaptil® to counter your dog's stress

The consequences of leaving your dog alone

If you do go out, your dog may become restless, feeling cut off even although it is still in familiar surroundings. It will not settle down and will become stressed. Certain types of dogs – notably the smaller companion breeds – are potentially most vulnerable to this type of issue, having been bred over the course of centuries to be around people.

It is important to be aware if your dog suffered from any display of separation anxiety previously, as often this can be a reason for people giving up their pets. Equally, if you are out for long periods, which would mean the dog being left on its own, then having a dog as a pet may not be the best choice, irrespective of its origins, for this reason.

In a bad case of separation anxiety, with your dog being able to roam freely around the home, there can be very significant damage, particularly to soft furnishings, with the seats of sofas and chairs being ripped apart, carpeting badly scratched or chewed, and curtains pulled down.

This topic has become a much more significant issue following the growth in dog-ownership linked to the recent Covid pandemic. Many people acquired puppies during one of several lockdowns, which meant that they were able to spend the day with their new pets, building a close bond with them.

Unfortunately, when things opened up again this meant many owners returned to their offices and spent more time on leisure activities

▼ Your dog needs to know that you are coming back. Absences of variable and unpredictable length will help to accustom your pet to being left.

▼ Taking your dog out regularly is vital, and timing this so it coincides with just before you need to leave your pet alone can help to settle it down to sleep.

▶ *Always allow your dog into the garden before going out, so that hopefully, it will relieve itself there and not soil indoors in your absence.*

away from the home. As a result, their dogs found themselves on their own for much longer periods than had previously been the case. This sudden realignment of life has triggered very many cases of separation anxiety, with some being severe, to the extent that owners are now giving up their dogs to rescue centres for this reason. This generation of 'lockdown puppies' will continue to present serious issues for rescue organizations stretching well into the future, especially given the overall growth in the dog population.

If you find that your lifestyle has changed, there are an increasing number of options available these days, to help you integrate your pet into it successfully so that it should not develop signs of separation anxiety. Some advanced planning will, however, be necessary, so that your dog can adjust to this change in routine.

Seeking assistance

It is possible that you might have a friend who can look after your dog for periods during the day. It should hopefully be possible to leave your dog for periods anyway, so it will not need constant companionship. Older dogs that naturally tend to sleep for longer during the day are most likely to settle down in your absence, compared with a young and boisterous puppy.

Another alternative may be to arrange for a dog walker to take your pet out when you are not around, which will break up the day for it. There are specialized businesses now offering dog-walking services, and it is important to do your research in this area. You must be certain that the person concerned has plenty of experience when it comes to working with and handling dogs. Equally, you need to establish how many dogs will be taken out together. If your pet is particularly nervous or aggressive, then this may not be the best option, certainly until you have had the option to build up a bond and get on top of these issues.

Another possibility can be to book your pet into a doggy day care centre. These are represented in many major cities today, and as their name suggests, they are somewhere your dog can go and will be looked after while you are at work. Once again, it is a good idea to check out the facilities and see if they correspond to your dog's needs, particularly if your pet suffers from any form of disability.

These centres can sometimes be a bit overwhelming for older dogs too, but for young, energetic individuals, they represent an ideal opportunity to get plenty of exercise during the day alongside other dogs, which

◀ *If your dog becomes bored, it may chew items around the home, with shoes being a popular choice. Provide toys that can be chewed instead.*

▶ *Prolonged absences may lead to wider-scale destruction in the home. It is advisable to restrict absences to short periods at first, monitoring how your dog reacts.*

▲ *It helps to get other family members involved in your dog's care, so that it will not feel so isolated when you are away.*

▲ *You can use home cameras to monitor what your dog is doing while you are out, to see if your pet settles down.*

means they are also useful for socialization purposes as well. There tends to be no long-term commitment, so if you are happy after seeing the premises and meeting some of the staff, it will probably be worth trying to see how your pet fits in for a few days, before taking any decision on whether this could represent a long-term option.

A further possibility, of course, could be to find someone who may be willing to come and sit with your dog and take it out while you are out during the day. Home-sitting services may be able to help in this regard.

Getting your dog used to being left alone

Nevertheless, it is important to pre-empt the risk of your dog developing separation anxiety from the outset, by teaching it to accept being left on its own for periods of time. It is always a good idea to take your dog out for a walk first, or at least let it have a run in your garden, so that it will then be more inclined to settle down and go to sleep.

Make sure that everything is comfortable for your dog, and it may

be best to put the bed in the kitchen, where your pet can potentially cause less damage than if it starts to become destructive elsewhere in the home. You may want to prepare though, by putting up a shield of acrylic sheeting over the lower area of the kitchen door, so your dog cannot inflict any damage with its claws by scratching.

Make sure there is a favourite chew toy within easy reach, and a bowl of water. Start by closing the door, leaving your dog here, and head off to another room. Stay away for perhaps a quarter of an hour, and then return to the kitchen to see if your dog has settled down to sleep. Hopefully, this will have happened

once the home went quiet. Do not worry too much if for a few moments, you hear your dog walking around, as hopefully, it should settle down quite quickly in these surroundings. Repeat this exercise randomly at various stages during the day, and for different periods of time, going out when you need to for brief intervals. If your dog

▼ *If you must be away from home regularly, you may need to use a dog-walking service, as a way of exercising your dog.*

▲ *It is hard to predict what may draw your dog's attention to chew around the home if it becomes bored when left on its own.*

back of the property, away from noises on the street which may distress your dog when it is on its own, triggering episodes of barking.

▲ *Keeping your dog confined in a crate and providing a comfortable bed will protect furnishings and furniture from damage.*

appreciates that you are coming back, this should provide reassurance and if it is settled down before you head off, this will also be helpful.

When you start going out, pause by the door for a few moments to listen to see whether your dog starts to bark. One of the advantages of confining your dog in the kitchen is that this room is often located at the

▼ *Let your dog see members of the family going out. It should soon realize that this is quite normal, and they will return.*

Preventing accidents

When they are teething around six months of age, young dogs will seek out items that they can gnaw on to soothe the associated discomfort and pain. It is particularly important to provide suitable toys that they can use for this purpose, offering a range of items, particularly if you going to be absent for a period of time. You also need to remain alert, though, because your dog's attention may be diverted by a piece of electrical cabling lying on the floor perhaps, or a wooden chair leg for example. It is especially important at this stage to make sure that all cabling is out of reach as far as possible, with plugs switched off so that if your dog does chew cabling, then there is no risk that it could electrocute itself. Should you spot your dog with cabling in its mouth at any stage, be sure to double-check the plug is off before removing the cabling from your pet's mouth, because otherwise, you could both end up being electrocuted.

Setting a routine is important right from the outset, to ensure that your dog does not soil in the home for

example. Always allow it out into the garden every two or three hours, and before you go out anywhere, thereby hopefully avoiding any accidents that will otherwise await your return.

In most cases, accidents happen because the owner was not observant enough, and failed to recognize their pet wanted to go out. Dogs are instinctively clean and will not soil in the home out of choice. If you encounter a persistent problem with a young dog that urinates regularly in the home, it will be worth seeking veterinary advice, as it could be suffering from a rare developmental abnormality causing urine to pass directly from the kidneys out of the body, bypassing the bladder.

Alternatively, urinating more frequently than normal could be indicative of cystitis. This infection of the urinary tract, which is more common in bitches than male dogs, will require veterinary treatment. It can explain an unexpected breakdown in toilet-training, with an affected dog suddenly urinating more frequently than usual.

Coping with visitors

In a way, a more direct form of separation anxiety is an issue with visitors, whether friends or people who are going to be working in and around your home. It is really a question of what is normal behaviour regarding a potential stranger turning up at the door and what is unacceptable. As with all discipline matters, establishing a routine and being consistent are the priorities.

It is quite usual for a dog to alert you by barking at the presence of someone knocking on the door in the first instance, just as if there is an intruder. What you want though is for your dog then to stop barking, and head away into another room where the door can be closed, allowing you to deal with the visitor.

Being alert

Some dogs get quite excited by the arrival of the mail or indeed a newspaper being delivered, sometimes leaping up to seize the items as they come through the letterbox. This needs to be prevented, because your dog could inadvertently catch the fingers of the person dropping the item through the door.

▼ *Some dogs may continue to bark when visitors turn up. Its behaviour will depend a lot on how used your pet is to meeting new people.*

The simple solution is to keep your dog away from the front door at times when deliveries are likely, thereby preventing this issue arising.

It is important to remember that the hearing of dogs is far more sensitive than ours, to the extent that they can detect sounds that are inaudible to our ears. It is therefore not fair to tell your dog off, when it may have a genuine reason for barking, such as hearing someone walk up a gravel drive or the sound of another dog barking in the distance. But what you do not want when someone turns up to see you is for your dog to carry on barking persistently throughout the visit. Once again, sound basic training will help to address the issue, by teaching your dog to go into a set room, such the kitchen, when someone knocks at the door. You can then close the door, and with a bed here, your dog should soon settle down.

▲ *You want to train your dog to greet a visitor, and then to sit down quietly without interfering in your conversation.*

People vary in their responses to dogs, and of course, they too are individuals, and will bond more easily with some people than others. When friends are visiting, then it may be possible to let your dog come and say hello; this is good for teaching socialization. After a brief initial period of excitement, your dog is likely to become bored and may wander off elsewhere or sit down quietly with you, with a little encouragement.

No jumping up!

When a friend calls round, especially someone whom your dog recognizes, it will be excited initially, and may jump up to say hello. This is not something to be encouraged however, because this can be

▶ *Dogs can sometimes prove to be a problem – both with visitors and family members – by patrolling around a table, in the hope of getting any pieces of food that are dropped.*

dangerous, if your dog behaves like this towards an older person or a child, as they could be knocked over, while the risk of muddy paws and snagging on clothing is ever-present with this type of behaviour. It can also be a serious issue in a park for example, if your dog rushes up to a stranger, and grabs a food item by jumping up in this way.

As always, it will be easier with a young dog to teach it to behave properly, but equally, it is possible to train an older individual to desist from jumping up as well. What you want to do is to persuade your pet to sit on the ground instead, in the same way that you don't want it pulling on the leash while walking, when meeting a friend outdoors.

Another reason that dogs jump up is often a combination of attention-seeking and boredom. This can frequently happen when you stand up and are about to head off to give your dog its food perhaps, but may be distracted by a phone call, so you remain standing in one place. Your dog then reacts in this way to check that it has not been forgotten.

Irrespective of the cause, however, ignore your dog when it behaves in this way, and step back, so that it can no longer support itself against your body as it jumps up. As always with training, clear unambiguous instructions are needed, and aside from verbal communication with your pet, visual signs can serve to reinforce the message. It can therefore be a good idea to remove any doubt in your dog's mind as to what is required by opening the palm of your hand and moving it in a downward direction while you tell your pet to 'sit'.

Eating with friends

Where you may have more of a problem is if you are eating, as your dog will probably be keen to share some of the food and may sit beside the table 'begging' for food. Ignore anything the dog is doing and if you need to distract your dog while you are eating, simply provide it with a suitable chew that will occupy it through this period. Keep ignoring the dog and once it realizes that it will not be receiving any titbits, then it should go off on its own.

◀ *Small dogs especially can feel left out when you are talking with a friend and seek to attract your attention by jumping up.*

▶ *Dogs are most likely to start trying to acquire food at the table if they are given titbits during meal-times. This is some-thing that should never be encouraged.*

Some concerns of modern living

Your rescue dog may have been living in the rescue centre all its life and may have never experienced a modern home where there is an abundance of electrical devices to encounter. In some respects, technology can be helpful, allowing owners to keep a check on their dogs when away from home, via a webcam, but on the other hand, technology can create bad habits too.

Electrical equipment

Many dogs are scared by the noise some of our electrical equipment makes in the home. In particular, dogs find the noise from vacuum cleaners very disturbing and will bark repeatedly when you are trying to clean the floor, frequently lunging aggressively towards the cleaner.

Try to introduce your dog to the vacuum gradually, allowing it to head to another part of the home if it wishes. Placing a treat on the vacuum is a technique that can desensitize a dog to the noise, so it realizes that it has nothing to fear. Leave the machine out so your dog can sniff around it, to become familiar with it. If your pet finds it particularly alarming, it is obviously better to plan

to avoid conflict by cleaning when your dog is elsewhere, either in the garden or out on a walk.

Distressing viewing habits

A common but very disruptive issue is if your dog acquires bad television viewing habits. Interestingly, some

▲ *Vacuum cleaners are something that tend to be disliked by many dogs, and they will sometimes resort to biting at the vacuum head.*

dogs express no interest in a television screen at all, while others become transfixed by it, whether they have grown up with a screen in their lives or not.

This is a relatively new problem, that has come about thanks to advances in technology. Back before the advent of flat-screen televisions, the old-style cathode ray tube sets simply resulted in an image that dogs could not make out clearly.

Modern sets with refresh rates of 100 hertz or more allow dogs to see the picture, and a television channel to appeal to dogs has even been set up on this basis. Whether you should encourage a dog to watch television

▼ *Some dogs can become transfixed by television, and often bark at dogs shown on-screen, and may even attempt to jump up at them.*

▶ A remote control will fit comfortably into a dog's mouth, and it may also have lingering scents of food associated with it, enhancing its appeal to your pet.

is another issue, because they will need to be discouraged from barking at the screen!

Dogs are most likely to respond to the sight of other dogs on television, especially if they are barking, but other animals too can be a source of interest to them, so any programmes involving wildlife could potentially be an issue. Dogs are particularly adept at picking up any on-screen movements, and they can still see well when the room lights may be turned down. They also have acute hearing of course, picking up on noises, even if to our ears the sound of a dog barking in the background of a film is barely audible.

One of the reasons that some dogs can react so intensely to on-screen imagery is that they are puzzled and confused by it. They can see and hear another dog, triggering two of their senses, but the third significant way in which dogs obtain information about their environment – through scent – is totally missing.

Boredom may also come into play, and if you are in the middle of a box set binge, your dog may feel that it needs to do something to get your attention. Dogs become very knowing in this regard, especially smaller individuals, and if your pet learns that starting to bark while you are watching television is guaranteed to achieve this aim, it will resort to this tactic. It is a difficult problem to solve, other than trying to get your pet to sleep under a light cover, as

clearly you do not want to have to shut it out of the room. Early action is recommended, before it becomes a deep-seated habit.

The tools of technology

The other thing that can happen in some cases is that your dog will steal the remote-control handset. Placing temptation out of reach is the best solution, because apart from hygienic concerns, there is an issue that aside from destroying the unit, and possibly choking on some of the components or cutting its mouth, your dog may also be exposed to the batteries within. If the batteries are damaged, they are likely to leak battery acid, which is extremely corrosive and will burn the inside of its mouth, and should the damaged batteries be swallowed, it could have horrendous consequences.

This is therefore a situation where you need to persuade your dog to drop the remote, and if necessary, be prepared to open its mouth and take the item away from it. Alternatively, you will have to bribe your dog to drop the remote by offering a tasty treat.

▶ Never leave charging cables or electrical flexes switched on, as these will be dangerous if they are chewed.

The same situation can sometimes arise with mobile phones, especially if yours is accommodated in a soft leather case. A phone will fit quite easily into your dog's mouth and is often left lying around within easy reach. Young dogs will perhaps be most likely to steal phones when teething, but always try to avoid leaving temptation within easy reach and invest in a hard case.

You need to be careful that you do not become reliant on using treats persistently in these instances, however, because of the risk that your dog becomes conditioned and will start stealing small household items ranging from shoes, glasses and mobile phones to obtain treats. As a rule, you want to reinforce good behaviour with rewards while discouraging bad behaviour.

Travel precautions

Cars feature prominently in the lives of many people today, and as such, dogs need to be accustomed to travelling in this way. Not all dogs, however, are instinctively happy going on car journeys, and you may need to be patient with your pet. This is an area where training is especially vital, because even a momentary distraction caused by your pet could have very serious consequences.

As mentioned previously, making sure that your dog is adequately restrained in the vehicle is essential, but initially, this can be very upsetting to your pet. Once again, much will depend on its background, because a dog that previously lived in a home and regularly was taken out in a car for walks will have no difficulty in terms of adapting to this type of lifestyle. However, an older dog that has hardly ever travelled in a car before is likely to require much more coaxing to relax.

Experiencing car travel

It is a good idea to take a young dog in particular out for short drives. This will allow it to experience car travel, and you can see how things go. It is possible that your dog may be car-sick, so avoid doing this just after a meal, as that will make the situation worse. It may be best, if you are using a dog guard, to be sure there is a lining tray in place as well,

so that if the worst happens, it will be relatively easy to clear up.

Drive around for a short time, and then allow your pet to have an opportunity to relieve itself, before heading home. What you do not want to do, however, is always to take your dog out in the car and give it a walk. Otherwise, you are likely to find that it becomes conditioned to this routine and tends to be more excitable than usual when travelling in the car. This may result in the dog

▲ *Dogs may sprint off unexpectedly, often following a scent, but never make the mistake of running after your pet. Call it back to you if possible.*

repeatedly barking, and not settling down. It can also contribute to increased protective aggression, should you park up on the way, and your dog spots another dog walking alongside a car. This may even spill over into aggression towards people who you talk to from the vehicle, with the window open, being manifested by uncontrolled barking from your pet.

If you step out of the car, leaving your dog within on its own, it may display this type of behaviour towards passing pedestrians as well. Although often dogs like Rottweilers, whose ancestry is partly based around guarding property, may be most inclined to behave in this way, even small companion breeds can react in a similar fashion.

◄ *Although dogs can often be reluctant about travelling by car at first, once they learn that this often means going out for a walk, they can be keen to get going!*

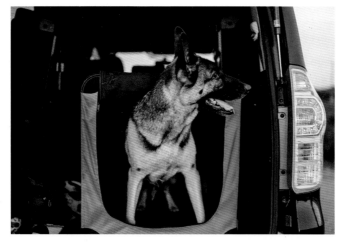

► *It is a good idea to put your dog on its leash before letting it out of the car, so that it cannot run off or into the path of any oncoming traffic.*

Care must be taken when opening the car to avoid your pet running off, which could be very dangerous. The excitement of being out in the open will often encourage a dog simply to run off initially, and it may travel some distance before stopping. It is critical not to compound the problem at this point by giving chase, as your dog will almost certainly be able to outrun you and will see it as a game.

Try to remain calm and call your pet back to you, hoping that it responds, or simply walk off after it. Hopefully, it will slow down after the initial burst of speed, and even if you cannot get that close, if you can get its attention, throw some treats and hopefully that will allow you to walk up and be able to put it on the leash.

Making plans
There are various steps that you can take to make travelling more relaxing for everyone in the car, including your dog, by offering it a chew by way of a distraction, if it barks repeatedly. Puzzle chews can be especially useful in this situation, as the dog becomes pre-occupied with releasing the hidden chew.

Some dogs prefer travelling in a crate, rather than being free behind a grill in the back of the car. This affords a greater degree of security

perhaps, and certainly after a period of exercise, your pet may even curl up and fall asleep here. Simply add a familiar piece of bedding from home, which has your pet's scent on it to make it feel more at home.

Another possibility, which can be especially useful with a large dog, is to fit sunshades to the car windows on the sides of the vehicle where the dog is travelling. This will serve to block off much of the dog's view, helping to prevent dogs and people that would otherwise be in its field of vision being so conspicuous.

Travel sickness
Virtually all dogs will take to travelling in cars over time, without become distressed, especially once they appreciate that they may often effectively get a reward at the end of the journey, in terms of a walk. But there may be some that continue to suffer from car sickness, which will be unpleasant for you and them, so contact your vet for advice. There is medication that can be provided, and over time, the problem should resolve itself, as the dog becomes more used to this type of transport.

There are other over-the-counter canine remedies that you can buy as well, which can be helpful in cases where your dog is simply nervous

about travelling and is not inclined to settle down. You can choose from various treatments which can help to make the trip less stressful. These can be especially useful if you are heading off on a long journey with your pet.

Tablets are again available, some of which may require a veterinary prescription although alternatively, you may find that a herbal remedy, typically incorporating the herb valerian, will suffice. Always read the instructions for use carefully, however, and don't give more than one type of tablet, unless your vet recommends this approach.

There are also calming sprays and diffusers on the market, which should help your pet to settle down. These have different constituents, but those containing calming dog

▼ *Never allow your dog to travel with its head out of the window. Aside from the risk of being hit, it is likely to end up with sore eyes.*

◄ Do not forget to take a water bowl and a container of water for your dog, so that your pet can have a drink after a period of exercise, or indeed, when you break your journey.

pheromones tend to be regarded as the most successful. Pheromones are chemical messengers that we cannot detect, which are transmitted through the air, and register through the Jacobsen's organ, an area in the roof of the dog's mouth which conveys the scent to the brain. Always choose a product of this type based on canine pheromones, however, rather than those of other species such as pig, as these generally give the best response.

Providing reassurance

You should also aim to make the actual journey as comfortable as possible too, by keeping the temperature reasonably cool, although if you open a window, be sure that your dog will not be in draught. Never allow your dog to ride with its head out of the window, as this can easily trigger an eye infection and is likely to be fatal if it

encounters a tree branch or object that the car is passing at speed.

One often-overlooked reason why dogs can become restless on a longer journey is that they are thirsty, so you should always take a supply of fresh drinking water and a bowl along for your pet. There are very convenient water bottles that can be used as drinkers which are ideal for this purpose. Try to stop every couple of hours or so, so your dog can stretch its legs and relieve itself, but do not allow your pet off its leash for a run, as it may not be so keen on coming back when called in unfamiliar surroundings.

It may be worth keeping an eye on the weather forecast before you

set off on your trip, because if you encounter a thunderstorm, your dog could become exceedingly upset, confronted both by thunder and lighting, as well as the unfamiliar sensation of being in a vehicle. You may need to pack a ThunderShirt® for your dog if the forecast is bad. It is important that you choose the right size, and you will need to measure your dog carefully as well as having a clear idea of its weight. The jacket is in effect a piece of clothing, fitting around the body. It is useful for nervous dogs, helping many of them to cope better when confronted by stressful situations. The way that it works is that it gives reassurance, exerting gentle pressure all over the body when it is being worn. It is made of a breathable, lightweight material, and so should not make your dog feel too hot.

Do not leave your dog in a car

Given that the temperature within a car can literally rise within minutes to a fatal level on a hot day, you must never, ever leave your dog alone in a car for any reason whatsoever, even if you are just popping out for a short time. Having the window partly open will not be sufficient to ensure your pet's safety.

◄ Special clothing, such as this ThunderShirt®, can help dogs to overcome their fear of thunder and may even help a nervous dog with other fears, reflected in separation anxiety and constant barking.

► *Start by travelling with your dog at a quiet time of day, when there will be fewer people around.*

Travelling on public transport

This is not something that nervous dogs will relish, especially at first. Therefore start by taking your pet by public transport at a time of day when there are likely to be fewer people travelling. This reduces the danger of your pet being accidentally trodden on or tripped over by fellow passengers, which will be less apparent in amongst a crowd. The risk is greatest in busy thoroughfares, such as at stations when concourses and platforms are crowded.

Before setting out on your journey, allow your dog to relieve itself. Dogs are most likely to adapt well to travelling on a bus, but especially with a smaller dog, pick up your pet and carry into the vehicle, in case it has difficulty mounting the platform, or is nervous. Choose a seat away from other people at first, especially children who may add to your pet's

stress by wanting to stroke it. This approach will give your pet an opportunity to settle down and get used to the unfamiliar sensations of the journey. If you undertake regular bus journeys with your dog, then it will soon become used to the experience, and will be unfazed by it.

If you have to negotiate going up or down escalators, and with a small dog in particular, pick it up if possible so there is no danger of your pet getting stuck by a claw, and panicking. It can be a good idea to introduce your dog to the experience of being at a station on occasions, before you get on to a train together.

It is vital that your dog walks well on the leash with you and will not pull away, causing a potential hazard both to other station users and itself. Always aim to keep your pet on as fairly tight leash therefore. Once you are on the train together, chose a quiet spot again, where your dog can see well and will also be out of the way of other people.

If you have a small dog and are concerned about whether it will become very distressed on the journey, not having travelled with you before, it may be worth using a travelling crate for your dog instead. Here it can feel relatively secure.

◄ *Keep your dog close to you when walking across busy travel concourses. This lessens the risk of someone falling over your pet.*

► *Once used to the experience, dogs will relax sufficiently to sit down on the floor alongside you for the duration of the journey.*

Outdoor concerns

Taking your dog out for a walk is necessary at least once if not twice a day, and dogs inevitably get excited by this experience. Regular walks are important for their physical health, helping them to maintain muscle tone and stop them from becoming overweight. They are also important for your pet's mental wellbeing too, allowing it to investigate and learn about the world around it.

Even before it is safe to let your dog off the leash, it is still vital to take it out for walks. One of the key issues that can crop up is that in its excitement, your dog pulls ahead when you go out for a walk. This can be dangerous, both for your dog and you, and it is important to be in control, especially if you have a large, powerful dog. If it rushes ahead, and the ground underfoot is slippery, your pet may even pull you over, causing you to lose your grip on the leash. The result then could be that your dog may run out into traffic, or you could end up with a fractured ankle, making it difficult to get back to your vehicle, let alone drive home.

▼ Remember that if you let your dog off the leash in unfamiliar surroundings, it may disappear and get lost.

◄ Dogs that spend most of their life in a city will be confronted by a host of new scents and experiences when taken out into the countryside for exercise.

Using a head collar

A dog that is constantly pulling ahead will also be likely to be panting and could injure its neck. This is because a collar offers little control, and so you may need to opt for the safety of a head collar, which resembles a horse's head collar, if other attempts to curb your pet's exuberance fail.

The point of contact in this case is on the underside of the chin, rather than on the neck, and it extends over the bridge of the nose. In the same way that a puppy will try to remove its collar at first, so an older dog fitted with a head collar will probably react in a similar way, by pawing at it, but this phase should soon pass.

Do not suddenly put the head collar on your pet and expect to take it out for a walk. You should allow the dog to become familiar with it beforehand, wearing it around the house, and then walk your pet around the garden by its head collar, as a first stage. It is important not to rush these initial stages, because you do not want your dog to become alarmed by the head collar.

Remember that your dog's ordinary collar or harness with its identity medallion stays in place, with the head collar being separate. Initially, it is a good idea to let your dog walk as before, using a collar and leash, and it can just wear its head collar at the start. Then

▲ *Always make sure that you keep your dog close when out for a walk together, even if your pet is off the leash at times.*

▶ *Maintain your dog's attention when out walking in the countryside, just as you would in the town.*

subsequently, by having a connecting leash attaching to both, this will ensure that you have more control of your pet, especially if it manages to slip out of the head collar for any reason.

A head collar will also help to prevent your dog pulling away from you across a path for example, which can be a particular problem if there are other people walking here. Ideally, you want your dog to walk just a step behind you, in a straight line. Even with an ordinary collar, you can practice this at home, so your

▼ *A canine head collar: check out the options and choose one of the correct sizes for your dog. Those that attach to the leash behind the head are preferable.*

dog becomes familiar with what is required, as well as at dog training courses.

Training your dog to walk correctly

You will need a wall of some sort or fence line which you can walk along, to stop your dog pulling away from you. Keep these sessions short – say a maximum of five minutes – but carry them out frequently, several times every day. Vary the routine too, by incorporating other lessons that your dog will hopefully have mastered, such as 'sit' or 'stay', into the session, replicating what will be required when you are out walking together.

Try to ensure that your dog remains focused on you, rather than being distracted by what else may be occurring within the vicinity. It is quite useful, once your dog has an appreciation of what is required, if there are other things happening around you in the garden, simply because out on the street, there will be other distractions too, and you need your dog to concentrate.

Patience is very important during

the training process, especially with an older dog that has received little training when it was younger. This is because dogs generally learn better early in life, but it is certainly possible to teach an older dog successfully: it just takes longer and requires more effort, but it can be immensely rewarding too!

Things become much harder when you first let your dog off the leash, but if you have carried out the preparation carefully, then the risk of any problems will be reduced. You need to be sure that your dog has good recall and will come back to you when called. It should also stay and sit readily for you.

Always bear in mind, however, that even if your dog proves to be a star pupil, both at home and as part of training class, it is likely to be less responsive once you let it off the leash. That is why choosing a safe and ideally relatively confined area for this purpose is vital. The most common problem that may arise is that of your dog disappearing. As mentioned, calling it back to you regularly, and rewarding it with a

◄ *Always remember to praise your dog when it returns to you after being called. This should help to improve its recall.*

tasty treat, such as a piece of chicken, will help to prevent this occurrence. (For further advice on walking a dog, see page 169.)

Recall matters

A dog with a hound or field sports ancestry which detects a scent will instinctively be drawn to pursue it and is likely to fail to respond to your calls as it heads off into the distance. It is worth remembering that in most cases, however, your dog will return to you, although this is likely to be an unnerving period.

The key thing to do is not to race after your dog if it picks up a scent. This is because you are only likely to encourage it to run faster, as it sees your involvement as part of a game. Stand your ground and call your dog back to you. With luck, even if it has disappeared out of sight, it will not have gone far before the thrill of the chase has worn off, and it seeks to return for a treat.

In cases where your dog has gone further afield, it should still be able to find its way back to you. Continue walking down the path that you are

on, calling your dog, and hopefully it should rejoin you before long. Under these circumstances, praise your dog, because although it did take off, the most important thing is that it returned of its own accord.

During training at home, it is a good idea to play hide and seek with your dog if possible, so that it needs to find you when you are out of sight. This is a useful preparation should this situation arise when you are out walking.

Although they may not be able to run as fast as the long-legged hound-type dogs, members of the terrier group are potentially more likely to end up in difficulties, because of their size. They may venture underground and end up being trapped here in a tunnel. As always, be alert to possible risks, and aim to steer your dog on a path away from them, putting your dog back on its leash if necessary.

Recognizing conflict and friendship

Very occasionally however, conflict may arise, and if you find yourself in-between two dogs that are disagreeing violently, don't put your

▼ *It can be more difficult to keep control of your pet when it is off the leash and there are other dogs nearby.*

▲ *A dog on a leash is alert to other dogs in its vicinity and is potentially more likely to react aggressively if another dog comes running up to it.*

▶ *Notice the relaxed posture of these two, and the way that neither has its hackles (the hair at the back of the neck) raised.*

hand down to try to pull them apart. Instead, run off in the opposite direction with your dog still on its leash. This is the best way to break them up. You may be followed for a short distance by the other dog, but it will generally not wish to pursue the encounter further, considering that it has emerged victorious, having driven your dog away.

If you walk in the same park regularly, the chances are that your dog will strike up a bond with some of the other dogs that it meets, and they will run around together. There is usually no need to intervene in this situation, which will not be an aggressive encounter, but simply a playful one, as can often be seen by displays of play-bowing.

It is not a good idea, however, to start throwing a toy for your dog to chase after when there are others nearby, as it can then become a free-for-all, with possessiveness soon emerging, which in turn can lead to serious conflict. Much depends how well-socialized your dog was, while it was growing up, in terms of how it relates to others of its own kind.

WALKING IN THE CITY

The problems that you can encounter with your dog when outdoors are influenced partly by its background, and by the area concerned. If you live in a city for example, it will be very difficult to find an area to exercise your pet where there are no other dogs, unlike the situation in a rural area.

Not all dogs are particularly social by nature, and some are protective towards their owners. What is often overlooked in public parks where there are often several dogs being exercised at the same time is that dogs are likely to react differently to being approached, depending whether they are on a leash. Dogs that are naturally quite well-disposed towards other dogs are much more likely to respond negatively when constrained in this way, as the other dog comes bounding up.

This can be hard to deal with, although most encounters of this type are quite brief. Be prepared for your dog to pull in the direction of the other individual that is running free as it approaches, and possibly lunging at it. In most cases, there is no serious conflict, and the other dog runs away.

▶ *These two dogs are clearly not feeling friendly. Notice the aggressive demeanour of the one on the right, and how it is trying to lunge at the other dog.*

Aggression issues

Cases of aggression always need to be treated seriously, and an uncontrollable aggressive dog faces a very uncertain future. Aggression towards people is something that rescue organizations focus on very specifically when dealing with incoming dogs. Unfortunately, not everyone who hands over a dog into the care of a rescue organization will reveal the true reason why they are taking this course of action.

Aggressive behaviour may not surface straight away when you take a dog home but may only begin once an incident has occurred that has triggered an adverse reaction in your new pet.

Biting

This is a serious issue and one that is sometimes hidden from the rescue centre when a dog is brought in. Rather than say the dog has bitten a household member, which may condemn the dog to being put to sleep, they come up with another reason in the hope that it will settle better in another home. This might be true, especially as the dog will be subsequently neutered if necessary, lowering its level of aggression.

Such an approach also assumes that it finds itself in a home with adult owners who understand its needs, ensuring that it will not be teased by children, as may have happened in the past. Interestingly, dog bites are more common during

▲ *Before a dog is rehomed, the rescue will take steps to investigate whether an individual is likely to be aggressive.*

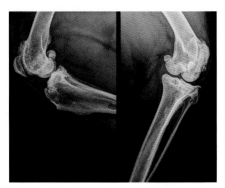

▲ *Joint ailments can cause a dog to strike out unexpectedly when it is being picked up, as it can be a painful experience.*

the summer heat, when a thunderstorm is on the way, indicating that dogs too may be less tolerant under certain circumstances.

There has been much discussion over recent years over 'breed versus deed', with so-called 'breed-specific' legislation having found its way on the statute books in various countries. Pit bull terriers (which are ironically not defined as a breed in the UK) and a small number of obscure other breeds, such as the dogo Argentino,

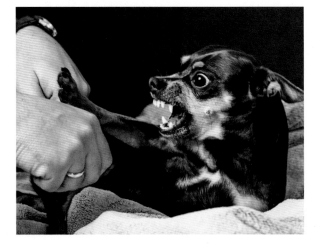

◄ *Size is no indicator of aggressive behaviour. Any dog in pain may strike out when being examined.*

Japanese toso and fila Brasiliero, cannot legally be brought into the UK or Australia for example.

It was not that there was ever many of these banned breeds being traded or kept – there was one Japanese toso in the UK for example when the country's dangerous dog legislation was enacted. Rather, there was a fear that these large mastiff-type dogs, with a reputation for fighting, could prove to be highly aggressive.

Dog bite statistics are often of little value though, simply because stating the number of people bitten by a particular breed of dog is misleading. What you need to know to gain a proper insight is not just how many bites were recorded against a particular breed, but also, how many dogs of that breed are resident in the country.

Today, although such legislation remains in place, there is a more enlightened recognition that biting

◄ *Assessments and keeping accurate records are an important part of the work of a rescue, so that those interested in rehoming dogs can be given a reliable overview of their dog's training responses.*

issues that can cause a dog to display signs of aggression, ranging from muscular injuries to brain tumours (although these are thankfully rare). Aggression can even be linked with the behavioural changes associated with hypothyroidism (see page 150), and it is therefore important to rule any medical issues out from the start.

and attacks on people can occur with any dog, although thankfully, serious incidents are very rare. However, displays of aggression by a dog are not something ever to be ignored, especially if there are young children in your household.

A dog recognizes the fact that the people who feed and look after its needs are in effect alpha leaders of the pack, and sees children as being lower down in the pack structure. It may therefore be more inclined to challenge a small child, rather than an adult.

Causes of aggression

There are several different reasons why a dog may prove to be aggressive, and it is very important to identify the cause, to try to find a solution. This is something that you should refer to the rescue centre to address, working with them to overcome the problem. If this is not possible, then you will need to seek out a good animal behaviourist who works in the field.

The starting point, however, should be to arrange a consultation with your vet. Providing as much information as possible about what happened at the time of the incident will help to identify the likely cause, including what you were doing in the period leading up to the incident.

It may be that your dog is in pain, and this triggered an uncharacteristic, aggressive response with no warning. This may have occurred typically when you tried to lift your dog, having previously had no difficulty in so doing. It could be developing arthritis, which has made it painful to be picked up, causing it to react aggressively.

There are various other medical

▶ *There are various causes of aggression in dogs, and if you find that your dog suddenly becomes aggressive at any stage, do not delay but seek expert advice. Such behaviour may have an underlying medical cause.*

Signs of concern

The degree of aggression that a dog displays will vary, but it is uncommon for an individual simply to lash out, unless it is in serious pain. There are likely to be a series of increasingly intense warning gestures, before a dog tries to bite, so it is possible to defuse a situation before it becomes a critical one.

Signs of stress that may not instantly be suggestive of aggression can include a dog licking its lips and yawning repeatedly. Its body posture will often appear more rigid, and its tail may be wagged much quicker than usual, acting as a visual warning.

▲ *Breeds such as huskies are more likely to be aggressive to other dogs, as they have a very strong pack hierarchy.*

▲ *In most cases, dogs do not become seriously injured in disputes, provided the weaker one can escape.*

Other behavioural changes may be seen in cases where the dog is acting defensively. Rescue dogs which have been badly treated, for example, may cower down with the tail tucked between the legs, especially if the individual is being backed into a corner. This is what is often described as fear aggression – the dog feels trapped and ultimately decides that it has no option other than to react aggressively, to defend itself. It will also look away, effectively indicating that it is not challenging you.

Growling, which becomes more intense, and drawing back of the lips to expose the teeth, are clear warning signs that should always be taken seriously. This can quickly escalate to the dog snapping with its teeth as it lunges forward. Behaviour of this type is often linked with possessive aggression – you may be seeking to take something away from your dog which it does not want to give up.

Interaction with other dogs

Raising the hackles – the area of fur on the back of the neck – is more of an overt challenge, especially if accompanied by intense barking. A dog uses this behaviour if it detects a possible intruder on your premises, and often inside cars, reflecting the fact that the dog is seeking to defend what it considers to be its territory. Raising the hackles helps to make the dog look bigger, by striking what is essentially an intimidatory posture.

Out and about, dogs may snap out at others that they encounter, or even strangers who seek to pet them. This is classed as social aggression, as it can often be linked back to poor socialization during puppyhood, with the dog not being familiar in communicating with others of its kind. It will be nervous and wary, causing it to act aggressively when challenged. Indeed, it is worth bearing in mind that many cases of aggression in dogs are not driven by a desire for dominance, but rather by fear.

How aggression can escalate

If a dog becomes frustrated in its immediate surroundings, typically being restrained here, when other things are happening in its vicinity and it wants to join in, then it is likely to become aggressive. This can occur when two dogs are challenging each other through a fence, and you want to get your dog to come in, so you bend down to grab its collar for this purpose as it is not responding, and then you end up being bitten.

Rather than attempt to do this

◄ *Never allow a dog to be teased, because it is then likely to become frustrated, and is likely to respond by displaying signs of aggressive behaviour. Children need to be supervised and taught how to play safely with a dog.*

▶ On occasions, one dog may be pursued by another, but ultimately, the chasing dog is likely to lose interest, and soon afterwards, the other dog will stop running.

though, make a loop with your dog's leash, passing the clip back through the loop, and then lasso your pet's neck, so you can drag it away. This is a much safer option to use if your dog is involved in a direct fight with another individual when you are out on a walk, than trying to separate them using your hands. If you are concerned that you are in a situation where you could be bitten by an aggressive dog, the best thing to do is to walk away from the situation.

Care needs to be taken when a young child is playing ball with a large dog, however, because if the dog jumps up at the child to try to seize the toy, it could quite easily knock the youngster to the ground and take the ball directly from the hand. This type of aggressive behaviour is potentially very serious of course.

THE RISK OF RABIES

Although currently not an issue in the UK or Australia, the risk of rabies should not be overlooked in other parts of the world. Indeed, if you are working with stray or rescue dogs in areas where rabies is known to occur, then you should be vaccinated.

A dog suffering from rabies may initially appear quite placid, and even more friendly than usual for a stray, not displaying the usual caution of a typical street dog for example. It may even allow you to stroke its fur. Unfortunately, however, the potentially deadly rabies virus will be present in its saliva, and it is a myth that you need to be bitten to develop rabies from an infected dog.

Direct contact which allows its saliva to enter a cut, which is quite possible if it licks your hand, will be sufficient. In fact, before they enter the terminal aggressive phase of this illness, rabid dogs are potentially more dangerous to people, simply in terms of transmitting the virus, because they do not appear to represent a hazard.

If you have been in this situation with a dog that is likely to be suffering from rabies, you need to get urgent medical attention as soon as possible. Wash the injury with clean water and soap initially and apply either an iodine- or alcohol-based disinfectant afterwards. Provided that you have a course of the rabies vaccine as soon as possible before symptoms of the infection develop, then you should survive, but if not, the prognosis is bleak.

The length of time for symptoms to develop is very variable, often taking anywhere from 3–12 weeks, although it can be sooner, depending on the part of the body where the bite occurred. A bite on the face, closer to the brain, is likely to lead to the infection developing much faster than if you are bitten on the foot. Given the risk to human health, rabies vaccines for dogs tend to be mandatory in several areas where the infection is present.

▼ Stray dogs represent a real risk of transmitting rabies to each other and people too. Without treatment, this viral infection is fatal.

Behavioural or health concerns

There can be times, especially in the early days, when it is unclear whether your dog may be suffering from a behavioural issue, or if the cause of your dog's problem could be an underlying illness. A health concern can in fact often be first manifested by a behavioural indicator. Paying close attention and getting guidance from your veterinary clinic for any changes in behaviour is vital.

It is worth getting into a routine of giving your dog a health check by looking at its eyes, to check that it is not blinking, and there is no discharge, leading to tear-staining down the side of the face nearest the nose. The coat itself should be healthy, with a good gloss, with no bald areas evident, nor should your pet be scratching or nibbling intently at its fur. Repeated scratching of an ear can be a symptom of an infection there, while bad breath is frequently indicative of a kidney complaint.

▲ *A dog that is reluctant to move and displays no interest in its food is likely to be unwell.*

▲ *If your dog will allow you to brush its teeth, this can help to prevent a build-up of tartar, leading to dental problems.*

Dental issues

When a dog is teething, around the age of six months, this will be a painful experience, and so it is again more inclined to prefer wet food, although, dogs do not actually chew

▼ *Tartar can be seen accumulating on this dog's teeth. It causes inflammation and erosion of the gum-line, and this in turn weakens the teeth in their sockets, making it painful for the dog to eat.*

their food to any significant extent but will simply gulp it down as quickly as possible. In some cases, especially with Chihuahua bloodlines, young dogs do not always lose their milk teeth, and so as their permanent teeth emerge, this can create what is effectively a double row. It is worth just checking on this if you acquire a young puppy, because this is something that needs veterinary attention, with the milk teeth having to be removed.

If you spot that an older dog is having issues eating, perhaps favouring one side of its mouth when picking up food and dropping it again on some occasions, this could be indicative of a long-standing dental issue. Dogs tend not to get cavities in their teeth as we do, but plaque builds up at the juncture between the tooth and the

gum. If left unchecked, the gum-line starts to erode, causing the tooth to loosen and infection to gain access.

Therefore, it is very important to check your dog's teeth regularly, and also to brush them, using a special canine (not human) toothpaste and brush kit for this purpose. Bad breath can be an indicator of dental issues in dogs, but there can be other causes, such as chronic kidney disease which is common in older dogs.

Becoming overweight

Weight gain in dogs is frequently insidious, and it is often linked to overfeeding combined with too little exercise. This problem is something that can often creep up unexpectedly and explains why it is important to weigh your pet regularly, as this is the best way to spot that it is starting to pile on the pounds.

◄ *Not all dogs are keen on or well-suited to running. Bulldog-type breeds particularly move at their own pace.*

► *If your dog becomes very tired after exercise, arrange a veterinary check-up, in case there is an underlying problem.*

Behavioural issues may be contributing to the problem. It could be that unbeknown to you, your pet is being slipped food regularly by another member of the household, and/or that too many treats are being handed out to the dog too often. It is especially important to watch this during training, as it can easily happen at this stage, and clearly, your dog is not running free and burning up as many calories as would otherwise be the case.

Certain breeds and resulting crosses are more inclined to put on weight than others, with size or background not being especially significant in this respect. Pugs, English bulldogs, Beagles, Labrador retrievers and Rottweilers and crosses involving these breeds can all be grouped in this category. Being overweight will restrict your dog's movement, potentially worsening cases of painful arthritis.

Panting in hot weather increases when a dog is obese, and particularly if it is brachycephalic (meaning that it has a compact, short nose), as in the case of a pug for example. This is because dogs cannot sweat like we do; they have just a few sweat glands between their paws. Instead, they cool themselves by panting.

Digestive upsets

A dog that has stolen and eaten something unsuitable is likely to suffer from diarrhoea. Yet the illness known as exocrine pancreatic insufficiency, which is especially identified with particular types of dogs, notably German Shepherds, will have a similar outcome. It appears to be a genetic illness, but thankfully, it can be corrected by supplementing the missing enzymes that would normally be produced by the pancreas which discharges these chemicals into the dog's small intestine, to assist the breakdown of its food. Whatever the cause of diarrhoea however, your dog will drink more than normal, trying to replace the fluid that it is losing from its body, so make sure that it can do so freely.

Other glandular problems can also result in diarrhoea, notably a malfunctioning in the output of the thyroid glands in the neck area,

▼ *Breeds like the German Shepherd dog can suffer from specific health problems. They may then need lifelong treatment.*

◀ *If your dog starts losing its fur, resulting in bald patches on its body, seek veterinary advice. This is not regular shedding and will need to be looked into. It could be a hormonal problem.*

resulting in the output of an excessive amount of the thyroid hormones, which serve to regulate the body's metabolism. Called hyperthyroidism, there will be other associated symptoms such as anxiety, which might also be a behavioural issue, although they have an underlying physical cause in this case.

Links between hormones, behaviour and health

The reverse situation – where there is an under-output of thyroid hormones – is called hypothyroidism, which is clinically the more common issue. The symptoms in this case are quite different, being effectively the reverse of when the hormonal output is too high. Again, this condition is insidious once onset. However, the signs of hypothyroidism tend to indicate some behavioural problems, with affected individuals sleeping for longer than usual, and appearing rather depressed. They also feel the cold, but again, you might attribute that to other factors such as age. Other signs may emerge, such as sporadic hair loss.

This is why it is always useful to take your dog to your vet, if you encounter any ongoing changes in behaviour. In the case of issues involving the thyroid glands, these can be resolved relatively easily, starting with some laboratory tests. It will then be a question of using a thyroid supplement, as prescribed by your vet, in cases of hypothyroidism. These will raise the blood levels back up to where they should be, reversing the physical changes that were apparent.

The situation with hyperthyroidism, which is rarer, is more complex, although your vet will be able to detect that these glands are enlarged. There is a risk of cancer though in such cases. Assuming this is not found, however, drugs that will inhibit the hormonal output can be used. It is worth pointing out that in cases where treatment for a confirmed case of hypothyroidism has started, a dog can start to suffer from signs of hyperthyroidism at this juncture, if the dosage level is initially too high.

Diabetes in dogs

Hormones are chemical messengers that balance the body's systems. The hormone insulin, which is produced in a different part of the pancreas, is vital to trigger the uptake of glucose sugar into the cells of the body, providing energy so they can function. Unfortunately, if there is an insulin deficiency, then the condition known as *diabetes mellitus* arises. Just as in people, the risk is increased when a dog is obese.

In the early stages, you may simply view this as breakdown in house-training, as your dog will urinate more frequently and often indoors even if only left for a short time. It will also drink more – never withhold water, as there will be an underlying reason if your dog is drinking more. You may also notice that it is keener than before to steal food, and yet is not very energetic.

Once again, these behavioural signs are indicators that the situation needs to be followed up with your vet, with an affected individual also

▼ Diabetes mellitus *in dogs is quite common, especially in older, overweight dogs. Treatment will involve dietary management and insulin injections.*

▲ *Congenital deafness is not uncommon in Dalmatians and affected individuals can find themselves in need of new homes.*

▲ *There is a high incidence of deafness in white boxers too. They are often regarded as unresponsive and disobedient.*

starting to lose weight. It is possible to test for diabetes, based on a urine sample, and treat the condition with daily insulin injections, combined with a special diet.

An unresponsive individual

Although it will almost certainly have been noticed previously and may indeed have been the reason that your dog passed into the care of a rescue organization in the first place, deafness can be an issue with some individuals, causing them to appear unresponsive and difficult to train. Once the problem has been identified however, it is possible to train affected dogs quite successfully, by focusing on hand signals.

Deafness in dogs can often be a genetic problem, linked to coat colouration or patterning. Dogs with piebald coats (being white with a darker colour) or pure white coats can often be affected, as may merles (displaying diluted colouration where blacks become blues) and roans (where there is white colouration running through the coat).

Congenital deafness is commonly seen in Dalmatians, with their piebald patterning, but as always, not all the puppies in the litter will necessarily be deaf. Also, the deafness may only affect one rather both ears, so an individual may not be totally deaf. It is obviously possible to arrange for your dog's hearing to be checked. The idea of clapping your hand just behind its head to see if it reacts is not adequate, because this creates air currents that your dog will feel on its face. This sensation rather than

▼ *It is quite difficult to determine whether a dog can hear, and sometimes, deafness may afflict one ear only.*

the sound may trigger a response.

It is still possible to build a close relationship with a dog that is partially or totally deaf, by relying on hand signals for communication between you. There are obviously dangers, however, given that a totally deaf dog will not be able to hear passing vehicles, and you will need to be particularly careful that it does not inadvertently step into the road when you are walking on the pavement.

CHAPTER SIX

HELPING OUT

Unfortunately, not everyone who would like to have a dog is necessarily in a position where they can share their life with one. Nevertheless, this does not mean that you cannot be involved with dogs and help to benefit their lives. It may be that you grew up in a home without a dog, and are keen to experience more about them, so that you can decide whether you should commit to having a canine companion of your own. Or, you may have a dog – perhaps one who came from the rescue – and you want to give something back for the companionship that your dog gives you. Volunteers come from a wide range of backgrounds.

There are also many different types of dog rescue, ranging from small scale operations working locally to others which operate internationally, while some of the better-known household names have nationwide rehousing centres. Irrespective of the type or scale of the rescue however, one thing that they all have in common is they depend to a greater or lesser extent on volunteers. Whatever your situation, your skills and enthusiasm can make a difference and will undoubtedly be appreciated by a rescue organization.

Aside from helping the dogs themselves, whatever role, or roles you take on, it also provides a great opportunity for you to meet new people with a shared interest, and broaden your social circle, making new friends as a result. It could even change your career path too, as you may decide that you want to train to undertake one of the increasing number of roles that involve working with dogs in one way or another today.

◄ Perhaps you already have a dog, or like dogs but are not in a situation where you can keep one yourself. You may therefore decide to help by volunteering to work at a rescue. Here you can apply your skills in a variety of ways and make new friends – both human and canine!

Volunteering

It is very straightforward to volunteer to help at a rescue centre in your neighbourhood. Start by tracking down those organizations nearby and then make contact. It obviously helps if you are aware of what the organization does before getting in touch, partly to show interest and commitment on your part, but also this may give some insight into the help that the rescue centre requires.

Each organization is likely to have a different application process that applies to volunteers. As a general rule, it is probably best to approach the organization concerned by email, outlining your interest, and particular areas of training or expertise that you could offer as a volunteer. It is also a good idea to give some indication of your availability, in terms of the hours that you could offer.

Avoid telephoning because firstly, staff are likely to be actively engaged in dealing with dogs, and secondly, it is likely that they will need time to direct your interest to the appropriate person in the organization who may not be on-site in any event. In the case of smaller organizations, which may be entirely run by volunteers, phone calls can take up their free time when they may need to be doing something else.

In these cases, where there are few if any salaried staff, the role played by volunteers usually needs to

▲ Manning a stand at in the street will help to raise both the organization's profile and funds.

be much more flexible, as a whole host of jobs will need to be carried out to ensure the smooth running of the operation. Roles in such cases tend to be quite interchangeable, with people being away at times and needing their regular work covered for example, while there may also be special 'one-off' events to plan for, such as stalls at summer fairs.

Fundraising

General administration skills are obviously very helpful when helping out with a fundraising event, such as being able to design flyers to hand out at events, not to mention larger posters. Pounding the pavements is the next stage in the process, asking local shops and other similar outlets if they will display publicity materials.

Then there will be other things like liaising with the event organizers, getting the display materials together and transporting them to the location, as well as agreeing a rota as to who is going to be on the stand and at what times. Importantly, decisions will also need to be taken about any fund-raising activities there, how best to take donations, and having some change as a float, with a cash tin on the day. With no public money available in most cases, rescues must raise their own funds, often relying on volunteers for this purpose.

◄ Increasingly these days, images for social media and publicity generally are in demand, serving to raise interest amongst supporters.

► Working behind the scenes on training is vital, helping to rehabilitate dogs that may not previously have had much contact with people.

◄ Well-socialized dogs often enjoy being at an event where they are the centre of attention, acting as a mascot for the rescue centre._

Publicity benefits

Coming up with innovative ideas to get publicity can be very important too. Good photography and videography skills can be exceedingly helpful for this purpose. Press releases are also an important way of persuading local, regional, and even national news media to run stories about the centre. In the case of bigger organizations, they have media teams and public relations companies handling this type of thing, but in small-scale rescues, this could offer an opportunity for you to develop your creativity.

Care does need to be taken, however, particularly with cases of ill-treatment, not to prejudice possible court proceedings that may be brought against those involved in the abuse. As with all such things, information given to the press needs to be well-organized, with the sign-off process clearly defined, and

► Some dogs generate more interest thanks to their cute appearance, but the right home still has to be found for them.

an ability to check not just the facts, but also what information can be given out.

Good publicity will also involve putting out helpful stories to benefit those who will be most interested in the work of the centre, in the guise of fellow dog-lovers. Those with a seasonal thread are often picked by local media, because unlike news-related reports, they do not need to be published instantly, but can be used as page-fillers on a quieter day when news may be harder to come by.

Stories related to dogs and summer heat, or what dog-owners need to think about when going on holiday with their pets are typically popular, being approved in advance and then credited to the rescue. These can really help to raise the organization's profile, especially if there is a web-link included at the end of the feature.

It is not just your skills that can be helpful, but also your contacts too. It may be that you know someone who will give the organization some publicity on a local radio station perhaps or has a large social media following and could assist, by promoting the rescue in that way. Cute photos of dogs are always popular, reaching canine enthusiasts right around the globe, raising awareness not just of dogs in need of new loving homes, but also, the rescue itself and its wider role, educating people about dogs and their care.

Hands-on help

Although it might not always be possible, because of health and safety issues or insurance concerns, you may be able to volunteer to help with the dogs that are in a rescue near you, assisting with their care on a regular basis. Usually, however, only people who are over 18 can volunteer, when working with the dogs directly.

If you want to take this step, the key thing is that you must be committed and reliable. Other people will be depending on you, and you will be working as part of a team. There will be form-filling to undertake at the outset, partly to check your suitability, and then there will probably be an induction day, which will allow you to see exactly what is involved.

It will not be a glamorous undertaking, cleaning kennels and runs out on a bitterly cold winter's day for example, and there will be an emotional aspect to this work too, which people at first tend to overlook in their enthusiasm. This is something that you need to consider – how volunteering could affect you personally. Things of course often work out very well, and there are many happy endings, with the rescue's dogs finding caring, forever homes and bringing a lot of joy to

▲ *Even when there is snow on the ground, the dogs will still need to be cared for and exercised as usual.*

those who take them on. Equally though, there can be heartbreak, seeing at first hand just how badly some dogs are treated, and there will be those that sadly are ill, and even with the best of care, fail to

recover, while others need to be euthanized on veterinary advice. Working effectively on the frontline with the dogs, you need to be prepared for these eventualities, upsetting though they will be to you. This is not a job for everyone, and it may be more appropriate for you to use your talents to support the rescue in other ways, instead of having a frontline role.

A range of tasks

Kennel-cleaning will probably only be part of the routine, essential though this task is, to the well-being of the canine residents. It may not necessarily mean going into the actual kennels themselves, but undertaking tasks in their vicinity, lightening the burden on any full-time kennel staff. This can extend from washing food and water bowls through to preparing food for the dogs. There are also likely to be other

▶ *Meeting members of the public interested in rehoming a dog is a critical and potentially time-consuming role, helping to match them carefully with the right dog and explaining why some individuals may not be suitable.*

▶ Interacting with the residents at the rescue is another key role that volunteers can undertake, particularly with those dogs which live there permanently, as they are unsuitable for rehoming.

tasks that need to be carried out, such as grooming and even bathing some of the dogs, often acting as an assistant under such circumstances.

One of the most significant tasks that may be undertaken by volunteers is helping to exercise the dogs. This activity needs to be carried out at least once if not twice a day, depending on the dogs, and their individual health assessments. If you are used to exercising dogs, this will be an enjoyable and very rewarding task – as well as a way of keeping fit yourself.

Taking the dogs out for walks is a key part of the work of the centre, and it can be a very time-consuming task, as they usually must be walked on their own. This also serves as a very good way of getting further insight into a dog's character, and its level of training, which you may be able to build on, when you are out together.

There are usually set routes that you follow in the vicinity of the centre. You may also need to take would-be adopters out with dogs as well, so they can become better-acquainted with their prospective new companion, and this time together will help to determine whether they are a compatible match.

Working with the dogs and as part of a team, you will be able to help formulate a personality guide for a particular dog. This in turn, when linked with whatever

background information has been passed to the rescue, will assist in giving a clear insight into the type of owner and home that would be most suitable for that individual.

Specific talents?

If you have maintenance and construction skills, these can be very useful, whether for repairing damage to a kennel through to creating secure outdoor runs for the dogs or ensuring the plumbing and electricity are working well. Gardening too may be important, creating a pleasant environment around the centre, as well as mowing the grass in general exercise areas.

Another very important hands-on role, which requires confidence, knowledge and diplomacy is home-checking, making sure that someone who is keen to take on a rescue dog has the knowledge and facilities for their choice of dog. It may be that another individual may be more

▶ Volunteers helping to walk the dogs every day eases the pressure on what is usually just a small number of full-time employees at the centre.

suitable for whatever reason, however, and this is something that will need to be conveyed without causing upset or offence.

A less obvious skill that may be very useful, in the case of rescue organizations that work in different countries, can be an ability to speak foreign languages. This will enable you to liaise with overseas contacts, and generally help to facilitate the smooth transport of dogs that will be coming to the rescue organization for re-homing, after passing their veterinary checks or into quarantine in some cases.

Fostering

Most rescue centres also rely on certain individuals acting as foster carers for dogs – these could be for hard-to-home dogs, or the rescue centre is simply full and needs to turn outside for help to accommodate dogs for a while. This is one avenue to explore if you are not quite ready to home a dog permanently and yet are looking to do something very rewarding.

It may be that you are not in a situation where you can take on a dog on a full-time basis, for a variety of reasons. It could be that you feel that you are at a stage in life where starting with a puppy again would be too much or it is too soon to make that commitment, having recently suffered the loss of a cherished elderly dog, and yet you seriously miss canine companionship.

A key role

Under such circumstances, fostering could prove to be the answer, and by so doing, this can bring a lot of advantages – not least that you are able to enjoy having a dog in your life again. Small rescues operating on tight budgets tend to rely significantly in some cases on

▼ *There can be times, especially if there is a large influx of puppies, that accommodation at the centre is stretched.*

foster-carers. The reason for this is partly financial, but even more significantly, dogs that are being fostered can benefit too.

A recent rescue centre study carried out in the Netherlands measured long-term stress levels in rescue dogs, by looking at the level of the hormone cortisol in their hair. This revealed that living in a well-run rescue is more stressful for a dog than being in a home environment, particularly for small dogs which are usually close human companions. This is why fostering can be so important, because as this study's results show, a dog's cortisol level will decline again, once it is back living in domestic surroundings.

One of the difficulties that many smaller rescues face is that their facilities are limited. If they take in a litter of 10 young puppies as an extreme example, this can exert serious pressure on the space that

they have available for other dogs. A rescue organization may have an informal arrangement with boarding kennels in the area who will help out in the event of an overspill, but obviously, these are businesses not charities, and will be charging a fee for their services, albeit perhaps below the market rate.

In addition, there will almost certainly be times when there is no space available at a boarding kennel at short notice, because they can become booked up many months in advance. This can often occur in the summer when many people are heading off on holiday, and around the time of festivities and public holidays, such as Christmas.

The benefits

Having a group of supporters who are willing and able to take dogs handed over into the rescue's care on such occasions is a huge bonus. It means that hopefully, the rescue will not become overstretched, and can continue to look after dogs in need. Clearly, when there is pressure on facilities, it will be a matter of assessing the dogs carefully and choosing those which are most suited to life in homes, typically having previously lived in these surroundings for example, rather than on the street.

Aside from helping in times of crisis, it is often the case that fostering can be of great benefit to the dog. As an example, this can

◄ If you can foster a dog, even if you cannot give it a permanent home, this will ease pressure on the rescue centre and allow the dog to experience living in a home – possibly for the first time ever.

apply in the case of an elderly individual, whose owner may have died. Having always lived within the confines of a home, such dogs would find it very difficult to adapt to suddenly living in kennels.

Equally at the other end of the age spectrum, puppies can benefit immensely from living in domestic surroundings early in life, as this helps to socialize them during the critical early weeks once they are independent. Work can start on house-training at this stage, making this process potentially much simpler for the puppy's subsequent carer, as well as helping it to settle more easily into its forever home in due course.

Not for everyone

Fostering can be very rewarding, but at the same time, it may not be practical for you, depending on your situation. If you are out at work for long periods or travel a lot, then the chances are that this will not be suitable for you. But on the other hand, if you have time to spare, and have plenty of experience with dogs, then this is something than could be ideal for your situation.

It is worth emphasizing the emotional demands of fostering, which means that it will not be ideal for everyone. Having to say goodbye to a dog that you have formed a bond with can be very difficult, and there is also the underlying uncertainty of how long a particular individual will be with you, which can make the whole process unsettling and challenging.

You can never be sure as a fosterer how long a dog will be in your care. It may only be a few days, but over a matter of weeks, you will find that you start to build up a close bond together, and then have to let go and say goodbye to your canine companion. This can be very upsetting and may make this key role exceedingly difficult for some people, particularly when, as inevitably happens, you have a dog that is a special character and forms a close rapport with you. By fostering, however, you can assist their transition, radically changing their lives for the better, in part by helping them to settle more easily in new surroundings which will hopefully prove to be their forever homes.

What to expect

When you take on a fostering role, it is very similar in some ways to taking on your own rescue dog, but there will be differences too. You will have some information hopefully about the dog's background, but from that stage onwards, it will also be a period of discovery, as you learn more about its behaviour, and how it responds to training.

One area where things will vary, however, should ideally be in the layout of your home. Ideally, it needs to be set up so the surfaces can be cleaned very easily, to remove the scent of previous canine occupants that have changed residencies and gone to new homes.

Otherwise, there is a risk that when a dog next comes to join you, it may start to try to superimpose itself by urinating indoors to eliminate the scent of the former resident, particularly if this dog had

▼ It may take a while to win the confidence of an individual that has been seriously mistreated by its past owners, and this is most likely to be achieved in a foster-home.

soiled on the carpets perhaps, leaving a lingering scent behind which another dog can pick up, but which we could not detect.

Getting prepared

Cleaning any carpeting thoroughly is therefore a good idea. A deep clean using a suitable canine product for this purpose is very important. Equally, all the bedding used by the previous dog must be washed, to eliminate any scent, or indeed, any trace of fleas. The food and water bowls must be disinfected thoroughly, as must any toys. These need to be of a robust design, and easily cleanable, rather than being of the soft toy variety.

Rescue dogs, especially in the early days, are potentially more vulnerable to acquiring infections, simply because they may have been neglected previously. They will also have been subject to unavoidable stress, having moved sometimes repeatedly from one place to another, encountering a range of totally new surroundings as well as people in a short space of time.

As always, it is obviously very important to give your new companion time to settle, and then,

◄ The difficulty of fostering is that even though a dog may have settled very well with you, it will need to move on to find another home in due course.

once it is fully vaccinated, you can start taking your dog out for walks. The management of your new companion will be influenced in part by its history. Clearly, an elderly dog will need to be looked after in a different way to a puppy, so you need to be prepared to be flexible in your approach.

Yet in all cases, the most important thing that you can do when fostering will be to help in building on whatever training the dog has had in the past. One of the best ways to boost a dog's confidence is to develop a routine, which will give stability to its life. It is vital to try to appreciate the dog's past life experiences. As an example, in the case of street dogs, you may even need to teach the dog to recognize and respond to its name.

Moving on

Inevitably, there will come a time when it will be necessary to part with your canine lodger, once it is found a permanent forever home, in which you may play a part, meeting and explaining the dog's temperament and requirements to those interested in re-homing it. When your canine companion moves on to a new home, it may leave a major gap in your life.

Hopefully though, you will be able to reflect on how you were able to assist in significantly improving the dog's quality of life, knowing that it will have found a loving home for the

rest of its life. Unfortunately, without any doubt, there will be another dog out there in similar need of your assistance, who will enrich your life significantly in the time that you are in contact together.

At some point, depending on your circumstances, you may even decide that a dog who comes to you to be fostered in the first place should end up as your forever companion. If this happens, the downside may be that it will be harder to foster other dogs in the future, although much depends on the temperament of your companion. A laid-back, friendly dog may be prepared to share its living space (up to a point) with others, and may help them to adapt to domestic surroundings where necessary.

▼ Weak or abandoned puppies may need handfeeding, and this is often best carried out in domestic surroundings.

Permanent residents

At most rescue centres – large or small – there are likely to be some dogs, who, for a wide variety of reasons, are not put up for adoption but end up becoming permanent residents at the centre. These too will need caring for, and although they will not be living in a domestic environment as such, they will still require plenty of fuss and attention.

The reasons these dogs are not suitable for re-homing are varied. It may often be because of their age or the fact that they have complex medical needs, which typically cannot be met in home surroundings. Some may also have difficult behavioural issues too, linked with their past, proving to be very destructive, for example.

It is also not uncommon for dogs whose owners have passed away to leave their cherished companions to a dog rescue organization, where they know their pets will be looked after well, for the rest of their lives. This often happens in cases where the person concerned has no family members or friends who are able to help out in this regard.

If you or someone you know finds themselves in this situation, the first stage will be to arrange a visit to the rescue, and discuss the possibility with them, to see if this is a viable option. If so, under most circumstances, the arrangement will then be formally written into your will and accompanied by a bequest to contribute towards your dog's care by your chosen rescue centre, with any surplus being used to assist other dogs in need. Obviously, it is important to take legal advice to ensure that your wishes will be met by the rescue centre.

Given the costs of running a rescue, fund-raising is critical, and many established rescues rely on legacies from generous benefactors

◄ There will be many different reasons why some dogs end up in permanent care at a rescue centre. Irrespective of their past experiences and current situation, they will need the same love and reassurance as any of the other dogs living there, so they can soon start to thrive in this environment.

to help them to meet their running costs, or use these for major projects, such as redeveloping or building a kennel block. If you feel that you would like to assist a rescue in this way, even by leaving a small gift, this is always very much appreciated. There may be tax benefits too, as far as the rescue is concerned, if it is set up as a charity.

Housing to look like a home

Some rescues even design the accommodation for their permanent residents not as kennels as such, but as rooms in a home, incorporating items such as chairs and sofas for the dogs. If you have such items to dispose of, that are past their best, then contacting your local rescue centre to see if these items would be of use to them may be a good idea.

Some rescues, even if they do not run a fund-raising shop as such, also have volunteers who will list

unwanted household items to sell online as another way of raising money for the organization. In either case therefore, your donation may help dogs at the rescue.

A star is born!

Sometimes, one of the permanent residents at the centre will take on a working role too, serving as a mascot and ambassador for the organization. Whenever there are special events that the centre is attending, such as a fair, or when visiting old people's homes, this particular dog will accompany whoever is going to represent the rescue and will probably get a lot more attention than they will! Dogs of this type can soon become much-loved figures within the local community too, and so they help to garner support for the rescue, as well as putting a smile on the face of everyone who meets them.

CHAPTER SEVEN

TRAINING

Rescue dogs can vary from those that have previously lived a feral lifestyle and have received no training whatsoever right through to well-trained individuals who are used to living in the home environment. Much therefore depends on the training that your new companion has had previously, in terms of what will be required going forwards. Even with a dog that has been well-trained however, you will need to build a bond in the first place by running through general training exercises, so that it learns to respond to you. This initial period will also provide the opportunity to establish areas where additional training will be beneficial.

When training your dog, it's best to start indoors in one room, then move to another room, then to the garden, and finish off by the roadside. The length of each training session often depends on which breed of dog you have, with sighthounds and terriers benefiting from frequent, short sessions, while border collies and labradors perform better with relatively long (and fewer) sessions. You may also have to take the age of your rescue dog into account when planning training sessions.

You should only carry out training when you are both in the mood for fun. If you are in a bad mood or your patience is low, stop. Do the same if the training is going wrong; don't get frustrated with your dog if it doesn't seem to understand what you want. We often talk to our dogs, and during training this can cause confusion. That is not to say that you shouldn't talk to your dog, but at this stage keep it to a minimum to avoid causing any distraction.

◄ *The amount of training that a rescue dog has received in the past may vary significantly, but all dogs can benefit from additional training, to help them integrate better into their new homes.*

Mastering the basics

There are basic instructions that all dogs must master, such as 'sit', 'lie down' and 'settle', and it is possible to teach new lessons to an old dog, although you will probably have to be more patient, compared with a puppy. Get your dog to respond immediately and you'll avoid having an overexcited, yapping, leaping hooligan every time you have a visitor, for example.

If during training you encounter specific problems, you can draw on the experience and support of the rescue centre staff. Simply explain the situation, and if necessary, the centre will be able to put you in touch with a trainer or a behaviourist who can work with you and your pet.

The following sequences will give some basic insights into how to train your dog. Try not to become over-reliant on treats as part of the training process however, as this can cause your dog to put on weight and become fixated on a reward. That is partly why clicker-training (see pages 74–5) is a better option.

▶ Teaching your puppy to sit when it is off the lead is important.

Training a dog to 'sit'

It is vital to get your dog to sit. This is generally not too difficult, because it is a natural posture. You need to get your dog to do it on command, at a time when it might be aiming to do something much more interesting, such as snuffling through the undergrowth following some unusual, enticing scent.

1 Have a few small food treats ready. Hold one in front of your dog's nose and move it upwards and backwards so that your dog's head moves up to follow the treat. As its head moves up, its hindquarters will go down. As soon as this area hits the floor, give a reward and praise your pet by name. If your dog begins jumping up at your hand, you are holding the treat too far away from the front of its nose.

2 Put your hand behind your back until your dog settles down. When you start again, make sure the treat is right at the end of its nose. As soon as your dog sits, you can offer another reward. Repeat, gradually increasing the time before the reward. The next stage is to make sure you say the word 'sit' as the dog is adopting the sitting position – not a second before .

3 Follow this up by checking that your dog understands what is required. Hide the treat behind your back and give the instruction to sit. Does the dog respond first time? If it stands looking at you, it doesn't understand, in which case you should go back to saying 'sit' as the dog assumes the sitting position. A dog will only have mastered the training when it sits immediately every time, on command.

Training a dog to 'lie down'

It is then a reasonably simple matter of getting your dog to lie down on command, from a sitting posture, although long-bodied dogs such as greyhounds may find this harder. The time to introduce the word 'down' is just as your dog is going into the correct position. Gradually increase the amount of time before you give a reward. After that, try getting your dog to lie down where there are minor distractions, for example in the back garden

1 Ask your dog to sit in front of you. When it is in the sitting position, hold a small food treat under its nose.

2 Slowly lower the treat down in a straight line from the dog's nose to its paws. While doing this, say 'down'.

3 As soon as your dog's chest hits the floor, praise your pet and offer a treat. Repeat the lesson several times.

Training a dog to 'settle down'

Having a dog that is able to settle down means that it won't be a pest when you are trying to eat a meal, that your dog will lie beside you when you have visitors, and that it will curl up next to you when you are reading. The more you practise this command, the easier it will get, and the longer amount of time your dog will stay settled.

1 Choose a time when your dog is tired, such as after a meal or a walk. Put your pet on a long lead and sit quietly.

2 Ignore the dog for a while. Do not say anything; wait it out. Eventually the dog should lie down by your side.

3 When your dog is settled, reward it quietly by gently stroking hits head. Offer a food treat and say 'settle down'.

Safety considerations

There are some commands that your dog needs to learn for its own safety. These include training your pet to come back to you every time when called, rather than running off. Other key safety commands are for your dog to be able to leave something alone and also to drop an object that may potentially be harmful to it.

Some dog owners think that just calling a dog by its name when your pet is off playing with other dogs will get an instant result. It won't. Calling like this means that when you use its name in future, it will soon associate that with the end of playtime and the walk, making the dog far less likely to return to you. So it's important when training your dog to come back to you that you use a suitable reward – one that compensates your dog well for being told to stop chasing other dogs. Ordinary dog biscuits will not be enough but a meaty morsel should work effectively.

Training a dog to come back

If your dog does not come back when called, it will have to be kept on a lead. This will reduce its social skills with other dogs and people, as it will not be free to interact.

Training should start around the home and then expanded to outdoors, perhaps using a retractable leash at first before letting the dog off the leash completely.

1 In a place with no distractions, feed your dog some tasty treats by hand, to get its attention.

2 Toss one small treat a short distance away from you, showing your dog where you want it to go.

3 While your dog is busy finding and eating a food treat, walk a few steps away from it.

4 When your dog has finished eating, call it. Praise your pet for looking up. In later repetitions, say 'come' at this point.

5 When your dog begins to run back to you, get really excited – smile, give it a round of applause and lots of praise.

6 As soon as your dog reaches you, reward it with a food treat and/or a favourite toy, then repeat the process.

Training a dog to leave an item alone

There will be many times in your dog's life when you'll want it to leave something or someone alone, such as an object picked up in the street, children's toys, joggers, cyclists or children playing in the park. A 'leave it' command covers all the items and people that you would rather your dog didn't touch, eat or chase. When teaching a 'leave it' command, let your dog decide what position it wants to go in. You shouldn't suddenly ask your pet to obey two commands at once, for example 'leave it' followed by 'down'.

1 Hold a treat in the palm of your hand under your dog's nose, then close your hand. Don't say anything.

2 Let your dog sniff, paw and lick. It will eventually back off. When this happens, say 'leave it' and provide the treat.

3 Next, make the exercise more difficult: put a few treats on the floor and ask your dog to 'leave it'.

4 If your dog sits patiently, reward it with a treat. Over time your pet will wait and look at you whenever you say 'leave it'.

Training a dog to drop an object

There are times when it is important that your dog drops an item that it has picked up, possibly because this could place it in danger. It is best to teach this is in stages. Use a favourite toy that can be used for tug, and some very tasty treats – the smellier the better. Offer your dog the toy and initiate a game of tug. Soon after, put a treat right under its nose, at which point it should drop the toy and take the treat. Your dog may take a couple of seconds to think about it, but bear with your pet. The crucial point is to say 'drop it' at the moment it drops the toy. Then show your pet the toy again and repeat. Teaching your dog to drop an object will make games of fetch fun.

1 Offer your dog one end of a tugger toy and initiate a game of tug-of-war, pulling the toy away from it.

2 Let go of the tugger and take a treat out of your pocket. Hold the treat right under your dog's nose.

3 Allow your dog time to decide what to do. Say 'drop it' as soon as it drops the toy, giving the treat and lots of praise.

Controlling your dog's movements

When you are out and about with your dog it is really important that you are in full control of its movements. Having the ability to stay where it is, to wait for you and to walk along beside you on a busy pavement will help to keep your dog safe and allow you both to have an enjoyable time together outside. Mastering these commands will allow your dog much more freedom when out and about.

Training a dog to 'stay'

The 'stay' command means 'stay where you are until I get back to you'. So, if your dog accidentally escapes out the front door and runs across a road, the wisest course of action is to tell your pet to stay where it is until you can get to it. Begin the training indoors, then move into the garden before going to a quiet place when out on a walk.

1 Begin by teaching your dog to remain still. Say 'stay' while holding up the flat of your hand.

2 Count slowly to five, and if your dog has not moved away, reward it with a small food treat.

3 When the dog can stay still for one minute by your side, begin moving away. Very slowly, take one step back.

4 Return and give your dog a reward, then gradually increase the number of steps. Always return though and give a reward.

Training a dog to 'wait'

There is a subtle difference between 'stay' and 'wait' commands. 'Stay' means 'stay where you are until I get back to you'. In contrast, 'wait' means 'we are going to do something else' and is more a case of good manners when you want your dog to keep quiet and behave, for example while waiting on the leash to cross a road.

1 Hold on to your dog's collar while you put a treat just out of its reach. Don't say anything at this stage.

2 Let your pet pull toward the treat while you hold its collar. When it relaxes and looks at you, say 'wait'.

3 Let go of your pet's collar and allow it to go and get the treat with praise for having waited patiently.

4 Practise the exercise until your dog can successfully wait without you having to hold on to its collar.

Training a dog to walk on a loose lead

Clearly, when you are going out with your dog, you need to be in full control, and this is especially the case with larger individuals that will pull more strongly and could cause an accident, such as tripping up a passer-by on a pavement. It is very important therefore that you train your dog to walk correctly on its leash. There are many training aids to facilitate lead-walking. If you have a strong dog, a harness is a great help, and a head collar will give you more control.

Start by training your dog to walk by your side without a lead on in this particular case.

▶ *Reward your dog when it obeys your command to 'walk close'.*

1 Begin by rewarding your dog for being at your side without a lead. Offer a small treat to get its attention.

2 As you step forward, pat the side of your leg and say 'walk close'. This is to let your dog know where you want it to be.

3 When your dog stands up and walks by your side, reward it with another food treat. Repeat this every few steps.

4 Once your dog can successfully walk by your side, carry out the same training procedure with a lead.

5 Pat your leg to show your dog where you want it. Do not pull on the lead; let your dog walk forward on its own.

6 Do not reward your dog for sitting. Wait until it walks calmly by your side with the leash hanging down loosely, then provide a treat.

Distance, duration and distractions

We need our dogs to follow commands, whether they are on or off the lead, in a park full of dogs and far away from you, or walking along the road by your side. We also need them to concentrate for the length of time we require. Your dog may already follow all your commands around the house but you also need to have the same level of control in other, more unpredictable situations.

When you are ready for this next level of training it is best to keep distractions to a minimum to begin with, and increase the duration of the exercises a little at a time.

Distance

When you begin training in a park where you have never done distance exercises before, start off with a series of short sessions of 'sit' while you walk a couple of steps away from your dog then come straight back. Use the environment as a reward. For example, if your pet is on a long lead, let it walk toward a tree for a good sniff. If your pet pulls towards something it wants without

sitting first, take a couple of steps back as a penalty and try again. When your dog gets it right, use rewards that it enjoys. Once your pet can sit successfully, stay and watch, let it off the lead and continue the training.

Duration

As well as increasing the distance between you and your dog, you can also begin to increase the amount of time between the desired behaviour and the reward. For example, vary the length of time that you stand back from your dog during a 'stay' command. On the first occasion, reward your dog after 25 seconds, the

next time 5 seconds, then 10 seconds. This will keep your dog guessing and, more importantly, it will make it try harder to get a reward from you.

Distractions

It's important to hold training sessions not just in classes but in the real world, with real distractions, because that is where your dog needs to obey you. Make sure your pet can walk on a loose lead without pulling forward when it sees a family member approaching. Can your dog ignore a toy on the floor when it walks past it, and sit while you talk on the telephone? Adding distractions is challenging, but worth the effort.

Working with distance, duration and distractions

1 When training your dog to 'stay', gradually increase the distance between you and your dog.

2 Also try increasing the duration of time between your dog's desirable behaviour and the reward.

2 Finally, add distractions to your training. For example, ask your dog to 'sit', then make a phone call.

Phasing out the reward

The ultimate aim of training your rescue dog is to get it to follow your commands whether you provide a reward or not. Whether your dog is a puppy or has never received any training you will need to reward and bribe it, but that state shouldn't exist forever. You can't keep stashing away rewards that will excite your dog (which soon becomes a practical problem), just to make sure it's obedient.

The use of food becomes bad psychologically: there's a very real danger that your dog will become too reliant on rewards and bribes, and will never obey a command without food. In addition, rewards can become boring over time, and the behaviour you want to encourage will gradually diminish. But at what point should you start phasing out food treats? The answer is as soon as your dog understands a command and can respond correctly with a treat.

Put your treats somewhere that you can reach them but your pet cannot, such as in your pocket or in a treat bag. Using the same hand movement that you used with the food lure, ask your dog to 'sit'. When it does sit, praise your pet profusely. Repeat the request several times, sometimes giving your dog a treat when it sits and sometimes not. There may be some confusion on your dog's part when you first dispense with the food lure, but bear with it. You may need to ask your dog twice to begin with.

When your dog manages to sit successfully without the food in your hand, you can now go on to rewarding the best responses. Make the rewards intermittent, only rewarding the very best responses and ignoring those that aren't as good. Use different rewards, such as a game of tug or throwing a ball, combined with verbal praise.

Improving training is all about getting the best out of your dog, so now is the time to ask more of it. Ask your dog to follow a few commands before you praise it – maybe a 'sit' and then a 'down'. Next, ask the dog to sit, walk ten paces away, then return and give plenty of praise. Then try asking it to sit, lie down and sit again, and then give a reward. Don't be too predictable with your training; ask for cues in different combinations and reward your dog at different times.

Delay the time your dog follows a cue and gets a reward. Ask it to sit, count to ten, then give a reward. Next time, ask it to lie down, count to five and then give a reward. You will get the best out of your dog if you keep it guessing. If your training is boring and predictable, your pet too will find it boring and predictable and you won't get the behaviour you deserve for all your hard work.

When you begin asking more of your dog, it may break its positions – your pet is used to being rewarded immediately, but you are changing the conditions. Don't panic; just put the dog back in position and try an easier task. If you were trying for a 10-second sit and your dog gets up, set it back and count to five instead. In time your pet will get it right, and its confidence will grow accordingly.

Phasing out food rewards

1 Hide some treats. Ask your dog to 'sit', using the hand movements you used before, but without any food.

2 Praise your dog when it sits. On some occasions give a food treat; at others, reward your pet with a game.

Index

A

abnormal appetite 119
abroad, rescue dogs from
  7
  health care/concerns 37
  homelessness,
    confirming 36
  identification 36–7
  older dogs 20
  'pet passport' scheme 37
  rabies vaccinations 37
  transport 36, 37
accidents indoors 65, 131
action toys 84
acupressure 108–9
acupuncture 108–9
adoption
  assessor's visits 44–5
  beginning the search
    34–5
  equipment needed 56
  fees 60–1
  first few days 62–3
  first meetings 42–3
  getting to know your dog
    46–7
  history of a dog 35
  older dogs 20–1
  paperwork 60–1
  puppies 18–19
  rescue centres 34
  safeguarding home and
    garden 50–1
age
  street dogs 12–13
  see also older dogs;
  puppies
aggression issues 144–7
agility courses 86, 93
appetite
  abnormal 119
  loss of 90–1, 116
arthritis 100
artificial respiration 104
assessor's visits 44–5
attention-seeking 116, 133

B

Bach flower remedies 112
bad breath 21
ball games 46–7, 124
  'drop', learning to 85
barking 132
baths 95
beds 57
behavioural issues
  body language 48–9
  dental issues 148
  digestive upsets 149
  first meetings 42–3
  hard to re-home dogs
    22–3
  health concerns and
    148–51
  hormones and 150
  overweight dogs 148–9
  street dogs 12–13
  unrecognised patterns
    40–1
  walks 47
bequests to rescue centres
  161
Bichons 16–17
bird food 45
bites (insect) 105
biting 144–5
bleeding 104–5
bloat 77
boarding kennels 97
body language 48–9
bonding with your dog
  46–7
boot liners 53
bowls for food and water
  56
breed rescues 34
buses 139

C

Canicross 87
carrying crates 53
cars
  arriving home from the
  centre 62
  experiencing 136–7
  on holidays 96
  leashes 52–3
  leaving the dog in 138
  mattresses 103
  ramps for 52, 102
  sunshades on windows
    137
  see also travel
cataracts 21
catching skills 86–7
cats
  in gardens, conflict and
    127
  living with 30–1, 66–7
cattle, contact with 80–1
CBD supplements 113
chairs, access to 63
chewing 19
chew toys 84
children 29–30, 62–3, 69,
  147
chiropractic 106
chronic pain
  acupuncture 108–9
  natural treatments 106–7
cities, walks in 143
claws 121
cleanliness, previous dog's
  scent and 45
clicker-training 74–5, 85,
  126
coats, issues with 148
coats for wearing outdoors
  57
cognitive functions 98,
  101
collars 56–7, 122
'come back', training to
  166
commercial feeds 88–9
countryside
  exercise in 80–1
  livestock, contact with
    80–1
  walks 76
  wild animals, contact
    with 81
countryside code 80
cow dung-eating 119
crates for travel 137

D

damage in the home 25
daycare services 65
deafness 151
death of owners 10
dental issues 148
designer dogs 14–15
diabetic dogs 11, 73, 90,
  95, 150–1
diarrhoea 149–50
diet see food and feeding
digestive health 91
digestive upsets 149–50
disabilities 102–3
documentation 60–1
doggy dancing 75
doggy day care centres
  129–30
dog-sitting services 25
dog-walking services 129
'drop', learning to 85, 124,
  167
dung-eating 119

E

ear issues 121
elderly owners 10
electric cables and
  equipment 50, 131,
  134
emergency situations 123
epilepsy 11
equipment
  coats 57
  collars and leashes 56–7
  disabilities 102–3
  food and water bowls 56
  outdoor 57
  sleeping beds 57

exercise
  agility courses 86, 93
  bloat 77
  co-ordination and
    catching 86–7
  GPS trackers 82, 83
  individual requirements
    77
  muddy dogs 79
  muzzles 76, 79
  obesity 93
  off the leash 78–9
  rural environment 76,
    80–1
  sport 86–7
  technology to help 82–3
exocrine pancreatic
  insufficiency 149
eyes 148

F
faeces-eating 119
feeding *see* food and
  feeding
fees, adoption 60–1
festive holidays 97
financial issues 10
  adoption fees 60–1
  assessing your
    commitment 26–7
first aid 104–5
first few days 62–3
first meetings 42–3
fitness 82–3
  see also exercise; health
    care/concerns
fleas 54–5
Flyball 87
flying disks 85
flystrike 103
food and feeding
  abnormal appetite 119
  appetite 90–1, 116, 119
  attention-seeking 116
  bowls 56
  commercial feeds 88–9
  dental issues 148
  eating with friends 133

fussy eaters 90–1
  gut health 91
  issues around 116–19
  loss of appetite 90–1
  meat diet 88
  nutrients 88
  older dogs 98–100
  poor past nourishment
    88
  possessiveness 117–18
  raw foods 89
  rubbish bins 119
  special diets 90
  supplements 89
  thieving 118–19
  two dogs 66–7
  vegetarian diet 88
fostering 158–60
fussy eaters 90–1

G
games 46–7
  ready to play body
    language 49
  see also toys
gardens
  cats, conflict and 127
  damage by dogs relieving
    themselves 65
  play concerns 124–7
  safeguarding 51
  supervision in 125
GPS trackers 82, 83
Greyhounds 15, 30
grooming 94–5
guards for cars 52, 136
gut health 91

H
handling problems 120–1
handover forms 60
hand signals 73
hard to re-home dogs
  commitment required 22
  damage in the home 25
  dog-sitting services 25
  help with 24–5
  permanent residents at

rescue centres 22–3
harnesses 53
head collars 140–1
health care/concerns
  aggression and 145
  arthritis 100
  artificial respiration 104
  back issues 102
  bad breath 21
  behavioural issues and
    148–51
  bites (insect) 105
  bleeding 104–5
  cataracts 21
  costs of 10
  deafness 151
  dental issues 148
  diabetic dogs 11, 73, 90,
    95, 150–1
  diarrhoea 149–50
  digestive upsets 149–50
  disabilities 102–3
  ear issues 121
  equipment 102–3
  exocrine pancreatic
    insufficiency 149
  fleas 54–5
  flystrike 103
  heat exhaustion 105
  help with 24–5
  history of a dog 35
  hormones 150
  hyperthyroidism 150
  incontinence issues 103
  insurance 61
  kidneys 21
  obesity 73, 82–3, 92–3,
    148–9
  older dogs 20–1
  overseas, rescue dogs
    from 37
  parasitic worms 54–5
  rabies vaccinations 37
  sight issues 20–1
  stings 105
  vaccinations 37, 54
  see also natural
    treatments

heat exhaustion 105
'heelwork to music' 75
holidays 96–7
homeless dogs
  number of 6
  reasons for 6, 10–11
  street dogs 12–13
homeopathy 113
home-sitting 96–7, 130
hormones 150
house-training 64–5
hydrotherapy 110–11
hyperthyroidism 150

I
identification 36–7, 97
incontinence issues 103
indoor accidents 65
indoor safeguarding 50–1
insurance 61

J
Jack Russell terriers 16–17
journals 59
jumping-up 132–3

K
kidney failure 21, 90

L
Labradoodles 14
lasers 110

leashes 122–3, 143
  car travel and 52–3
  lengths 57
  letting off from 71
  off the leash 78–9
'leave it', training to 167
'lie down', training to 165
life expectancy
  street dogs 13
  see also older dogs;
    puppies
life-stage diets 90
lifestyle, assessment of
  apartment life 31
  cats, living with 30–1
  children 29–30
  older dogs 15
  separation anxiety
    128–31
  work-dog balance 28
livestock, contact with
  80–1
lungworms 55
Lurchers 30

M
massage 106–7
meat diet 88
medical care/issues see
  health care/concerns
medication
  mouths, opening 95
  see also health care/
    concerns
microchips 36–7, 61, 97
mobile phones 135
mouths, opening 95
muddy dogs 79
muzzles 76, 79

N
names 61
national kennel clubs 35
natural treatments
  aiding recovery 110–11
  Bach flower remedies 112

calming your dog 112–13
CBD supplements 113
chiropractic 106
chronic pain 106–7
homeopathy 113
hydrotherapy 110–11
massage 106–7
osteopathy 107
physiotherapy 110
reiki 111
tissue salts 113
neighbourhood dogs 67
nervousness
  body language 48–9
  natural treatments for
    calming your dog
    112–13
  street dogs 12–13
neutering 6, 51
  puppies 19
  veterinary care 54
new people, meeting
  68–9
night-time routines 63
nutrients 88

O
obesity 73, 82–3, 92–3,
  148–9
off the leash 78–9
older dogs
  adoption 20–1
  arthritis 100
  bowls for food and water
    56
  cognitive functions 98,
    101
  food 98–100
  health care 20–1
  insight into 98
  issues with ageing
    98–101
  life-stage diets 90
  lifestyle changes 100–1
  teeth 148
  veterinary check-ups 101

weight 98, 101
orthopaedic mattresses
  103
osteopathy 107
other pets 66–7
outdoor safeguarding 51
overseas, rescue dogs
  from 7
  health care/concerns 37
  homelessness, confirming
    36
  identification 36–7
  older dogs 20
  'pet passport' scheme 37
  rabies vaccinations 37
  transport 36, 37
overweight dogs see
  obesity

P
paperwork 60–1
parasitic worms 54–5
paws 121
permanent residents 161
'pet passport' scheme 37
physiotherapy 110
pica 119
pigs, contact with 81
poodles 14
possessiveness
  food 117–18
  toys 125–6
probiotics 91
public transport 139
puppies
  adoption 18–19
  chewing 19
  life-stage diets 90
  neutering 19
  safeguarding home and
    garden 50
  socialization phase 12
  street dogs 12–13
  teeth 148
  training 19
pure-bred dogs 15

R
rabies
  risk of 147
  vaccinations 37
racing greyhounds 15, 30
ramps for cars 52, 102
raw foods 89
reiki 111
remote controls 135
rescue centres
  background information,
    providing to 38–9
  bequests to 161
  contacting 38
  first meetings 42–3
  fundraising 154
  permanent residents 161
  publicity 154
  types of 34
  visits, arranging 39
  volunteering at 154–7
Rescue Remedy 112
retrievers 16, 17
rivers, walks near 81
roundworms 55
routines
  establishing 63, 131
  house-training 64–5
rubbish bins 119
rural environment
  exercise in 80–1
  livestock, contact with
    80–1
  walks 76
  wild animals, contact
    with 81

S
scenthounds 16
sea, walks near 81
seat belts 53
separation anxiety 128–31
settle down, training to
  165
sheep, contact with 80
sighthounds 16

sight issues 20–1
'sit', training to 164
sleeping
 beds 57
 routines 63
slimming foods 93
snakes, contact with 81
socialization
 making time for 27
 puppies 12
sofas, access to 63
soft toys 43
special diets 90
specialist breed rescues 34
sport 86–7
Staffordshire bull terriers
 16, 17
stings 105
street dogs 12–13
sunshades on car windows
 137
supplements 89

T
tablets
 opening mouths for 95
tapeworms 55
television viewing habits
 134–5
ThunderShirt® 138
thyroid hormones 150
tissue salts 113
toys
 action toys 84
 chew toys 84
 drop, learning to 124
 flying disks 85
 garden play 124
 learning to drop 85
 plush (soft) toys 43
 possessiveness 125–6
 tug toys 84
 two dogs 66–7
trackers 82, 83
training
 assessing progress 74

basics 73, 164–5
beginning 72–3
clicker-training 74–5, 85,
 126
'come back' 166
communication 72
controlling dog's
 movements 168–9
distance 170
distractions 170
'drop', learning to 85,
 124, 167
duration 170
guidelines 72
hand signals 73
'heelwork to music' 75
help with 72, 164
'leave it', learning to 167
'lie down', earning to 165
loose lead walking 169
on-going 74–5
phasing out rewards 171
puppies 19
safety 166–7
sessions 73
'settle down', learning to
 165
'sit', learning to 164
'stay', learning to 168
treats 73, 74
'wait', learning to 168
trains 139
transport
overseas, rescue dogs
 from 36, 37
see also travel
travel
crates 137
on holiday 96
public transport 139
sickness 137–8
ThunderShirt® 138
see also cars
treats 95
phasing out rewards 171
training 73

tug toys 84
two dogs 66–7
types of dogs 14–17

U
ultrasound 110
urban environment, walks
 in 143

V
vaccinations
 rabies 37
 responsibility for 27
 veterinary care 54
vacuum cleaners 134
vegetarian diet 88
veterinary care
 costs of 10
 fleas 54–5
 neutering 54
 older dogs 101
 parasitic worms 54–5
 vaccinations 54
visitors to the house 68–9,
 132–3
volunteering
 fostering 158–60
 fundraising 154
 hands-on 156–7
 publicity 154
 at rescue centres 154–7

W
walks
 behaviour on 47
 bloat 77
 cities 143
 conflict/friendship with
 other dogs 142–3
 correct walking 141–2
 crossing roads 76
 GPS trackers 82, 83
 head collars 140–1
 muddy dogs 79
 off the leash 78–9
 pulling ahead 140
 recall 142
 from rescue centres 157
 rural environment 76,
 80–1
 technology to help 82–3
 water 77
 whistling 79
water bowls 56
weight
 obesity 73, 82–3, 92–3
 older dogs 98, 101
whistling 79
wild animals, contact with
 81
wild boar, contact with 81
work-dog balance 28
worms 55

This edition is published by Lorenz Books
an imprint of Anness Publishing Ltd
info@anness.com
www.annesspublishing.com

© Anness Publishing Ltd 2022

Publisher Joanna Lorenz
Editorial Director Helen Sudell
Designer Nigel Partridge
Additional dog training text Patsy Parry
Production Controller Ben Worley

A CIP catalogue record for this book is available from
the British Library.

About the Author

David Alderton grew up in a home surrounded by pets and
originally trained to be a vet at Cambridge University until an
allergic dermatitis forced a change of career in his final year of
study. Since then, David has used his experience, knowledge,
and passion for this subject to concentrate on writing about
pets and their care.

He has kept a variety of rescue dogs through his life, and
worked with both breed rehoming organizations and the Dogs
Trust – the UK's largest canine charity – in various ways, helping
to raise awareness about the number of homeless dogs in need
of permanent, loving homes.

David currently shares his life with two rescue dogs – Rose,
who is a lively three-legged, one-eared Jack Russell terrier, and
Dora, a Pomeranian-type dog, who was found in a paraplegic
state, and required months of care before she was even able to
start walking, let alone running around again.

David's books have sold almost 7 million copies worldwide
and are available in over 30 languages. He has won the
prestigious Maxwell Medallion from the Dog Writers'
Association of America. David is also well-known as a
columnist, writing for a variety of newspapers and magazines,
and broadcasts regularly on radio and television and via
podcasts. He is filming a series on pets, which will include
information about rescue dogs. His website can be found at
www.petinfoclub.com

Publisher's Note

Although the advice and information in this book are believed
to be accurate at the time of going to press, neither the author
not the publisher can accept any legal responsibility or liability
for any errors or omissions that may have been made nor for
any inaccuracies nor for any loss, harm or injury that comes
about from following instructions or advice in this book.

The reader should not regard the recommendations, ideas
and techniques expressed and described in this book as
substitutes for the advice of a qualified vet. Any use to which
the recommendations, ideas and techniques are put is at the
reader's sole discretion. It is the owner's responsibility to be in
control of their pet at all times.

Picture Acknowledgements
With thanks to www.shutterstock.com for supplying many of
the pictures. Page 138bl pic: ©2022 ThunderShirt®. Pages 175
and 176 supplied by the author. All other photographs supplied
by Anness Publishing Limited.